WAL ~~KS~~

and other activities
in
FINISTERE

36 circular walks with maps and directions
(and suggestions for 45 more...)

Researched, walked and written by
Wendy Mewes

Photographs and production by Harold Mewes

a RED DOG guide book

Walking and other activities in Finistère
published by Red Dog Books
ISBN 0 9536001 3 0

**For Rufus and Brian
who have
helped and hindered
in equal measure
on these and many other walks in Finistère**

Thanks to Richard Curtis of Brittany Sailing for the photograph
of his yacht Cornish Legend on page 124

Main cover picture - Monts d'Arrée

The right of Wendy Mewes to be identified as the author of
this work is asserted in accordance with sections 77 and 78 of
the Copyright Designs and Patents Act 1988

British Library Cataloguing-in-Publication Data
A catalogue record for this book is available from the British Library

Red Dog Books is based in Axbridge, Somerset and in Brittany.
Enquiries should be addressed to the editorial office at
Red Dog Books, 29410 Plounéour-Ménez, France.

email: reddogbooks@wanadoo.fr

www.reddogbooks.com

Printed and bound in Great Britain by
Bath Press Ltd, Bath

ABOUT THIS BOOK

WALKING

A passion for walking and the remarkable countryside in which we live have been the inspirations for this book, although selecting a limited number of walks from all those we have enjoyed here in recent years has not been easy.

Full directions are given for 36 circular walks of different types and varying lengths all over the department of Finistère. There are also 45 additional suggestions given in brief for good places to follow existing circuits or to make up your own walks.

The contents are arranged on a north, centre, south basis (see map inside the front cover) and each section contains four long walks of 12kms or more, four medium walks of 7–11kms and four short walks of 6kms or less. The routes have been chosen to provide a variety of terrain, views and sites of historical interest. They include town, coastal and rural routes, both hilly and almost flat, so everyone should be able to find something that suits their mood or ability. Some of the walks have many points of special note, whilst others rely simply on the pleasures of nature.

An overall length and rough timing are given at the beginning of each walk, together with location, parking and refreshment details, and a sketch map of the route. Please note that all distances given are approximate. The **key** on page 6 explains the grading of walks (Levels 1-4), map symbols and abbreviations used in the text.

Within many of the walks, short detours to special sites are given, with distances (not included in the overall length for each walk). These are self-contained excursions, which return to the point of departure and then pick up the main walk again. They are shown in the text in blue and on the maps by dotted lines. For other interesting places in the vicinity of these walks, see the Red Dog Guidebook: Finistère - Things to see and do at the End of the World.

Background information such as historical facts, legends and points of architectural or archaeological interest is given in brown within the text for each walk. The photos are intended to give a realistic flavour of the terrain in the main walking seasons, rather than to suggest constant sunshine.

The walks in this book are not complicated or difficult. Experienced walkers with good directional sense will be able to follow many of the routes from the maps alone. For those who prefer the security of words, I have tried to give very full directions, which will perhaps save the reader some of the many hours I have spent searching, debating and retracing my steps.

The best time of year for walking here is spring or autumn, but winter usually also has plenty of clear, fine days and is rarely very cold. None of the paths will be busy at these times, except near particular beauty spots, and the weather will not be too hot. Those walking the coastal path or the high hills should be aware that there is often little shelter from the sun or rain in these areas. When road-walking, remember to stay on the left facing on-coming traffic where possible.

Hunting in Finistère is not allowed on Tuesdays and Fridays. Otherwise, from September to February, it can take place on any day of the week, the most popular being Sunday and Thursday. It is rare, however, to meet a hunter on the main paths.

Finally, and most important of all, the timings given reflect the intended purpose of these walks - pleasure not endurance.

OTHER ACTIVITIES

The second section of the book provides basic information and contacts as a starting point for those interested in pursuing other activities in Finistère. Golf, cycling, riding, water-sports and fishing are the main topics included. The list of establishments is only a small selection of what's available, and please note that we do not claim personal experience of their facilities.

Opening hours will vary according to the time of year and it is advisable to phone to check before driving long distances in the hope of a game of golf or an afternoon's riding. Contact details are given and the map in this section shows the location of the various activity providers. Some are not open outside the main holiday seasons.

Readers' comments on any of the entries or suggestions for others are welcomed for future editions.

WENDY MEWES

CONTENTS

About this book 3
Key 6
Glossary 6
Introduction to walking in Finistère 7

WALKS
Long = 12kms+   Medium = 7-11kms   Short = up to 6kms

North Long
Dorduff estuary, Plouescat, Brélès, Le Conquet 9
North Medium
Le Relec, Saint-Méen, Lanrivoaré, Guisseny 22
North Short
Morlaix, Landivisiau, Landerneau, Lampaul-Ploudalmézeau . . . 33
North Extra Suggestions 44

Centre Long
Huelgoat, Monts d'Arrée, Tal-ar-Groaz, Ménez Hom 46
Centre Medium
Ménez Meur, Loqueffret, Châteauneuf-du-Faou, Camaret . . . 58
Centre Short
Carhaix, Châteaulin, Saint-Thois, Sainte-Barbe 70
Centre Extra Suggestions 80

South Long
Forêt de Carnoët, Combrit, Bay of Audierne, Goyen estuary . . 83
South Medium
Portec, Raguénez, Pouldreuzic, Pointe du Van 97
South Short
Pont Aven, Moros estuary, Stangala, Douarnenez 108
South Extra Suggestions 116

OTHER ACTIVITIES

Map 118
Golf 119
Cycling 120
Riding 122
Watersports 124
Fishing 126

KEY

MAP SYMBOLS

✧	archaeological or historical feature	♨	fontaine/spring
✳	belvedere/viewpoint	◊	menhir
⹀	bridge	⊓	dolmen
■	building(s)	ⵏ	lighthouse
Ⲁ	campsite	P	parking for start of walk
⊹	château	▲	peak
⌂	church or chapel	⼗⼗	suspension bridge
†	calvary or wayside cross	A	reference point in the directions
✩	fort		

GRADING OF WALKS (for guidance only)

Level 1 : fairly level route
Level 2 : fairly level route with gradual climbs
Level 3 : generally up and down, paths needing care
Level 4 : one or more very steep slope and/or many steps

ABBREVIATIONS

TO = tourist office
hs = high season, normally July/August
ls = low season, normally October to February
GR = long distance footpath

GLOSSARY

aber - estuary
bourg - village with facilities
château - castle or mansion
dolmen - ancient stone tomb
écluse - lock
fontaine - shrine over a spring
landes - moor

lavoir - washing place
marais - marsh
menhir - standing stone
passerelle - footbridge
ria - estuary
sentier - footpath
tourbière - peat bog

WALKING IN FINISTÈRE

Finistère is a walker's paradise, with an immensely varied coastline, the highest hills in Brittany crowning a well-wooded interior, and impressive rivers and estuaries throughout. Lighthouses, distinctive Breton church spires and Neolithic standing stones are constant landmarks in the changing scenery.

Water is never far away here, with the sea on three sides, and each coastline has its own attractions. In the north there is a singular quality of light, together with striking rock formations and wide inlets (abers). The craggy cliffs and vast sandy beaches of the west are pounded by Atlantic breakers, whilst the south is gentler and riven by fine estuaries (rias). A major footpath runs right round the sharply indented coastline, amounting to more than 1200kms of walking.

Of all the rivers, the most impressive is the Aulne, snaking its way right across the centre of Finistère, for a long stretch part of the Nantes/Brest canal, littered with locks. On a smaller scale, but no less beguiling, are the Élorn in the north and the Odet in the south. There are also the Réservoir de St–Michel, in its exceptional setting below the Monts d'Arrée, and nearby Lac du Drennec, both surrounded by walking trails and glorious views.

The interior of the department is divided by two ranges of hills (none over 400m) running roughly east/west. The high bleak heaths of the Monts d'Arrée in the north are criss-crossed by little-used tracks and afford exceptional views over central Finistère. By contrast, further south are the thickly wooded slopes and pretty villages of the Black Mountains.

Other remains of Brittany's ancient forests linger on the slopes around Huelgoat, where the river Argent tumbles over and tunnels under granite boulders of spectacular size and formation. In addition, well-managed forests such as the Forêt du Cranou and the Forêt de Carnoët provide straightforward and attractive walking trails.

There is also plenty of gentle rural walking through farmland and secluded hamlets. Most of the tracks alongside fields and through woods (ancient lines of communication between villages) are still communal land, and, unlike England, very few footpaths in this area involve crossing any private property. Country roads are still usually quiet enough for comfortable walking.

Towns also provide many stimulating walks, with routes of historic interest and hilly viewpoints. Those situated on estuaries often retain the fine buildings of their rich commercial past and elaborate religious establishments. Rural scenery is never far away even here: Douarnenez, for example, has the green acres of the Plomarc'h alongside its busy ports and from the centre of Pont Aven, a short stroll leads to wooded hills.

The best viewpoint of all, and a good hilly climb, is the summit of Ménez Hom, which on a clear day provides 360° panoramic views of the sea and coast, the hills and valleys of the interior, as well as the serpentine course of the Aulne estuary.

Walks in this book reflect the exceptional variety of the most unexpected and rewarding scenery in Brittany.

North	1 DORDUFF ESTUARY	Long

Length 13kms	Time 4hrs	Level 3

Location & parking: north of MORLAIX. From the centre, take the D76 along the estuary, then turn right to Ploujean and follow signs to the Château de Suscinio (now also an agricultural college). Park by the gates of the château with the college to the right.

Refreshments: none on route.

This is a glorious route along the Dorduff estuary, with views of the Bay of Morlaix, and peaceful river valleys. Inland sections meander through small hamlets and past ancient buildings such as the Château of Suscinio. Near and distant views across wooded hills enhance this walk, which does include many ups and downs and a couple of steep slopes.

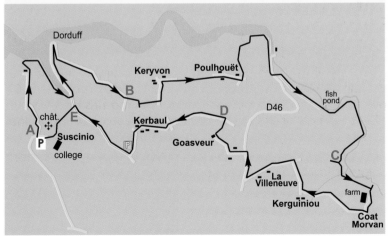

DIRECTIONS

The Château of Suscinio dates from the 17th century and once belonged to Cornic, a flamboyant corsair, well-known along the coasts around Morlaix and honoured by Louis XV. Today it is an agricultural college, whose members maintain the gardens, which are open to the public.

A **From the parking, walk back uphill a few metres and take the stony track on the right, along the low wall of the château grounds.**

At the end of the track, bear right down a tarmac road. When the track goes sharply left, turn off right into the woods, where a wooden board points left down a narrow path.

Follow this all the way down through the trees to the waterside. Care is needed on this path. At the bottom, turn right along the Dorduff estuary.

The path borders the estuary and then a creek. At the little tarmac road, turn left to go down the other side of the creek. This comes out onto a small quay on the Dorduff.

The road now turns uphill and inland. It is a steady climb, with good views behind to the bay of Morlaix. At the top, the track runs between fields with fine open views, including the Château of Suscinio to the right.

B **When the road bends to the right, leave it and go straight ahead on a sunken footpath between high banks.**

At the road, turn left into the hamlet of Keryvon. Follow the road round to the right and continue straight ahead to the hamlet of Poulhouët.

Soon after a long low house on the left, turn left down a grassy wooded track between banks.

At the river, turn right and follow the path ahead. At a little road, turn right to continue the walk (noting to the left a parking area with seat and good view) past a mill on the opposite bank. About 300m ahead, the track meets the main D46.

Turn right and walk carefully up this road – beware traffic – for about 200m. Then take a wide stony track on the left, and follow this to the river again, continuing past a fish pond and bridge. The path narrows here and starts to go up and down, with good views. Ignore small turnings off and keep to the main path.

C The path turns uphill and eventually reaches a T-junction. Turn sharp left downhill here. Cross the stream on a plank bridge and follow the path beside a river meadow.

At a T-junction of paths, turn right uphill, to the left of the farm at Coat Morvan (note the old house on the right) and at the top turn right.

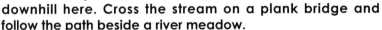

Continue ahead, with good open views over the Dorduff valley. At the hamlet of Kerguinou, follow the road round to the right. At a T-junction turn left, and continue ahead through Kerlapousset and La Villeneuve to the D46.

Turn right and walk along the main road - beware traffic - for about 200m. Take the first road on the left to Goazveur Izella and follow it through houses to the end, where a grassy track goes straight ahead along the back of a stone building. Take this path, which almost immediately turns right. Follow this and continue ahead to a road. Turn left.

D Follow this road bearing left downhill through Kerbaul with views across to the château and college. After 250m, at a parking area on the right, take the tarmac track to the right (marked no through road) along a stream valley.

E After about 600m, look out for an electricity tower on the left with stone steps up to it. Follow the woodland path up to the right of the tower. The château of Suscinio is on the right. Bear left at a junction of paths. Go straight ahead almost to the college buildings and turn right to the car-park.

Length 12kms	**Time** 4hrs	**Level** 3

Location & parking: from the centre of PLOUESCAT, take the D10 towards Cléder for one kilometre and then turn right on a small road signed to Gorrébloué, Kerzéan and the déchetterie. Follow this ahead for 1½kms to the Chapel of Kerzéan. Park by the chapel.

Refreshments: none on route.

There is much of architectural and historical interest in the form of châteaux, chapels, calvaires and former mills on this walk, as well as some fine long views to the sea, glorious beech trees and meandering streams in green valleys. There is also a good variety of tracks and paths, although some will need care in poor weather.

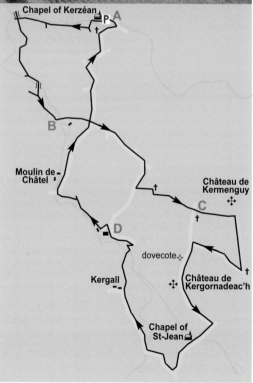

DIRECTIONS

A Take the grassy footpath along below the chapel and follow this over a stream. At a junction of paths, go straight on and then follow the path round to the right (signed Pont Pochard) along the valley.

At a major crossroads of paths, go left uphill, then to the right round the edge of a field. Stay on the path into the trees again.

At another major junction of paths, continue round to the left. Cross the bridge and then follow the path to the left. Where the path forks, bear left and continue ahead for about 500m.

B Then turn left to pass in front of the mill-house and continue uphill to the crossroads. Here, go straight on, still uphill. (Note the views of the sea behind). Where the road forks, go straight ahead. After the electricity tower, go right where the road forks and after about 350m, left on a track across a field towards a stone cross (calvaire). Follow the path round in front of it and then past the greenhouses.

The high plain of Léon has always been a rich source of vegetables, especially artichokes and cauliflowers. Brittany Ferries was started in 1973 specifically to transport this produce to neighbouring celtic markets in Cornwall.

C At the road, go straight on past another calvaire, to the gates of the (private) Château de Kermenguy on the left. Turn right here down an avenue of beech trees. At the end though the gates, go right along a track. At the road, turn left and continue past a dovecote and then the ruined Château de Kergornadéac'h about 450m ahead.

13

This château, one of the last in France to be fortified in this style, was built in 1630. It was deliberately destroyed by fire in about 1760 as the proprietor wished to force her son to court the king's favour at Versailles and not rusticate here!

Then continue ahead and turn right at the next junction. The Chapel of St-Jean is ahead on the right.

This medieval chapel was rebuilt in 1823. Dedicated to St-Jean, it was renowned for the curative powers of its sacred fountain. Many came to throw in coins in hope that the water would cure their eye illnesses.

Soon after the chapel, turn right (signed Moulin de Kerany) and stay on the same road for about 750m to the hamlet of Kergall. Where the road swings sharply left, bear right along a track round the edge of a house.

Follow this down to the stream, where it bears sharply left and then right again to join a little road. Turn left here.

D Follow the road round to the right past the farm and then sharp left just after. After about 80m, turn right along a grassy track which soon follows the stream. When the track forks, go left and continue ahead to the road.

Turn right uphill. (The Moulin de Châtel and the mill-pond are on the left).

At the junction bear left at the triangle and then straight on. There are good views of the sea and Plouescat from here.

Bear right at the next junction, and again at the next. Where the road forks soon after, go left to the calvaire. From here continue ahead and turn left over the stream to regain the chapel and the starting point.

Length 12½kms	Time 4hrs	Level 2

Location & parking: BRÉLÈS is off the D27 from St-Renan. Turn right just uphill from the church (rue du Stade) and there is a large lay-by to park in on the right after 200m by the sports field.

Refreshments: restaurant and bar in Brélès.

This walk has everything: good paths, green valleys, streams and lakes, wide tracks with open views, a château (detour), an exceptionally fine menhir, the Aber Ildut estuary and a very attractive starting place - the bourg of Brélès.

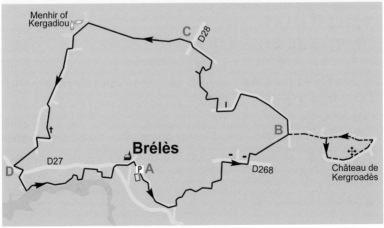

DIRECTIONS

A **From the lay-by, continue down the small road for about 600m. Shortly after crossing a stream, where the road bends right, go left down a wide track. Follow this all the way to the road (D268).**

Turn right (path by the side of the road) for about 300m and when the path ends, cross the road and take the green track opposite.

B **At a crossroads, turn left along a narrow road.**

DETOUR (2 x 1½kms): go straight across here for about 600m and then right at a junction of paths. Go left at the next junction and walk through the grounds  of the early 17ᵗʰ century Château de Kergroadès. (The house itself is not open to the public, but the path passes directly in front of the building). Continue ahead through the gates and bear left, then left again shortly after. Go straight ahead at the junction of paths and retrace the outward route back to point B, then turn right for the main walk.

At a junction, go left and stay on this road for about 800m. After a right hand bend, take the second path on the right.

Follow the path round to the left and continue ahead alongside a lake. Bear right along the top of it and then stay on the same path uphill.

At a major fork bear right and continue ahead to a small road. Turn left.

C **At the main road (D28), cross over and continue (a few paces to the right) along a foot-path for about 1.5 kms. Keep straight ahead on the same path. When it comes out on a track, turn left. Two menhirs, one fallen, are in the field to the right of this track. Continue to a junction of tracks ahead.**

To go right up to the menhirs, bear right here for a few paces and then in through a field entrance, where a path wiggles its way through the crop to the stones.

The sylph-like standing stone, the Menhir of Kergadiou is 8.75m high, one of the tallest in Brittany. According to legend, it was stolen from a witch in Scotland, who swore revenge. To destroy it, she hurled another, which fell short and broke in pieces.

At the junction, bear left and then right when the track meets a road. Stay on this for 1km and then, where it bends right, go ahead on a green foot-path, passing a stone cross on the left. At the road, go right and after about 250m, left at the next junction. After 100m, take a foot-path on the right.

D At the road (D27), go left, with care, for about 150m and then turn right (signed Sentier Côtier). Where this road bends right soon after, take the foot-path on the left down to the estuary (Aber Ildut) and bear left along it. Shortly after crossing a creek about a kilometre later, the path turns inland.

The dovecote in the field to the right of the path belongs to the Manoir de Bel Air, built in 1599, which is just visible as the path detours round it.

Turn right (up steps), parallel with the main road. Then follow the path across a track and to the right, back to the water.

After 150m, turn left over a stream after a wooden barrier and go on up to the road. Cross and then take the other road to the right back into Brélès. Go right just after the church to return to the parking.

Length 12½kms	Time 4hrs	Level 3

Location & parking: near LE CONQUET. From Brest take the D789 to Le Conquet. Shortly before the town, turn right on the D67 (direction St-Renan) and then left onto the D28 (Plage des Blancs Sablons) about 800m later. Continue on this road for just over a kilometre and then, where the road bends right, turn sharp left (direction Les Blancs Sablons). The car-park is off this road to the right about 600m ahead.

Refreshments: choice of restaurants/crêperies in Le Conquet.

This is an exceptional walk. The route begins alongside a beautiful beach and then goes right round the wild and unspoilt Kermorvan peninsula, with excellent sea views as far as the island of Ouessant. Crossing a narrow footbridge across the ria gives the opportunity of discovering the colourful harbour and centre of picturesque Le Conquet (good lunch-stop), before re–crossing the water for yet another change of scenery on the return through pine woods.

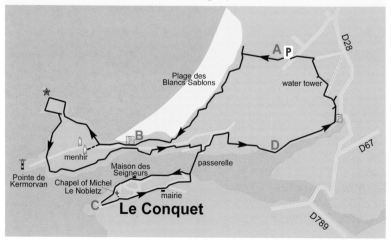

DIRECTIONS

A Take the path in the far left-hand corner of the car-park. Just before the beach, turn left along the coastal path which is fenced on this stretch. Follow this along the cliff towards the peninsula ahead. Where the path divides at some wooden steps, go down to the right and then ahead just above the beach.

In 1558, 10,000 English and Dutch soldiers landed on these sands and then sacked the town of Le Conquet. Out of 450 houses, only eight remained untouched.

Continue on this narrow path all the way to the car-park at the beginning of the peninsula ahead. (Tide permitting, it is possible to do this part of the walk on the beach, if preferred).

Across the water is the fishing port of Le Conquet. Most striking in this view is the Maison des Seigneurs with its three stair turrets on the back of the house.

B Go right, through the car-park, and past the wooden barrier up the narrow tarmac road ahead. After about 250m, take the coast path to the right.

DETOUR (2x125m): Just ahead up the tarmac road, one on each side, are two small standing stones (menhirs). Return to join the coast path.

Follow the narrow path right the way round the peninsula.

There are good views of the old fort on the island ahead. It is possible at low tide, with care, to walk out to it for a closer look.

Continue, going right where the path forks, to skirt a little cove, round to the Pointe de Kermorvan, where there is a lighthouse. The path crosses straight over the road here and soon begins to turn back towards the town of Le Conquet, across the estuary.

Go through the car-park and up the road for about 30m, then take the path on the right for a short loop along the estuary before rejoining the road.

Go right for about 250m to a line of houses set back from the road and turn down to follow the path running along directly in front of them. Where the path forks, go right downhill past an old stone lavoir.

Turn left at the bottom and then after about 250m, turn right, down a narrow route by a high wall to the passerelle.

Cross the bridge and then go right immediately on the coastal path. Bear right when the path joins the road and continue ahead all the way along the harbour area. Bear right along the rue Troadec in front of one of the finest houses in Le Conquet.

There are many ancient stone houses with exterior staircases and carved doorways in the harbour area. The fine Maison des Seigneurs was once used to store coal and water for the first steam ferry to the islands!

At an open square, continue to bear right (past a vehicle no-entry sign).

C As the road begins to drop down to the harbour before the jetty, go up the steps on the left and then turn left at the top back towards the town.

The road swings left and there is a little chapel ahead. Follow the road to the right before it.

DETOUR (of a few paces!): Chapel of Michel le Nobletz, a 17th century missionary in Finistère who used painted 'maps' (talennou) to bring religion alive to illiterate peasants. He is buried in the church at the top of the town.

Continue ahead along rue Clémenceau to the pretty centre of the town where there are good restaurants/crêperies in lovely old buildings. Go straight on past the Mairie, an elaborate mansion set back from the road on the right.

The mairie was built as a residence in 1859 by François Tissier, founder of a large iodine factory here. It was later used as the German occupation headquarters.

On past the Tourist Office, turn left (rue Amiral Guépratte) downhill to the passerelle and re-cross the estuary.

On the other side go up past the old wall and then turn right. Follow the road up to a T-junction, but just before it, go right along a narrow path by the finger-post. Where this ends, turn right a few paces ahead down a footpath. This bends left shortly after and continues down to the bank of the estuary.

D Here bear left along it and follow this path through fir-trees for about 750m. At the end turn left up through the trees immediately before a car-park near the bridge for the D67.

Go right where another path comes in from the left and then left uphill at a fork straight after. Go right at a wider track and then left immediately before a large water-tower.

After about 100m, bear right between wooden posts and continue ahead. When this track bends sharply to the right, turn left along a narrow path between banks.

At the road, the starting point car-park is just to the left.

North	5 LE RELEC	Medium
Length 11kms	**Time** 3hrs	**Level** 3

Location & parking: LE RELEC, south of Morlaix, 2kms off D769. Park by the abbey or in the village square.

Refreshments: restaurant in Le Relec; none on route.

This undulating walk starts in the wooded valley where the ancient abbey church of Le Relec stands. It includes a wide range of scenery from wooded paths and streams, old stone crosses and granite hamlets to the open heights of the Monts d'Arrée with far-reaching views. Most climbs are gradual but there are plenty of ups and downs on this route. Off the beaten track, it should be mainly quiet and peaceful, even in high season.

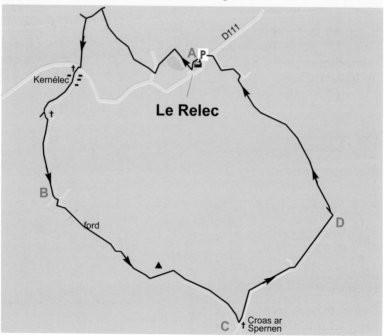

DIRECTIONS

The abbey was founded in 1132 by Cistercian monks. The Romanesque church, with its impressive night stair and clock, is well worth a visit.

A From the car-park at Le Relec, walk past the abbey to the village square and then up the footpath beside the lake.

At the top turn left and follow the path to a minor road. Turn left and then after about 50m turn right up a path at the side of a small cottage.

This beautiful tree-lined path between ancient banks climbs steadily uphill, becoming steep for a short stretch, followed by a gentle descent to a junction. Turn left here.

This wider path goes downhill to an open grassy junction. Turn left here.

The path goes uphill again and then down to a road. Turn right and almost immediately left down the footpath by the stone cross.

The signals mast on the top of the Monts d'Arrée is visible straight ahead on the horizon here, and Roc'h Tredudon.

The path goes down through the attractive hamlet of Kernélec. At a fork, bear left over a little stream. At another calvary, bear right.

B At a junction on the open hillside with many paths leading from it, bear left and then right at once by a post with a small green metal plaque (arrow to Croas Ar Spernen).

Looking back at the second calvary

Cross a ford over a stream and then climb steadily towards the

23

rocky crests. Stay on the stony track bearing right up the hill and then to the left as it nears the peak. Parts of this path are very boggy. Aim for the wooden posts marking the way, and then bear left towards the peak.

The path goes straight along behind the peak and then curves to the right, gradually descending towards plantations of fir trees. This long path eventually comes out at a minor road, with the base of a stone  cross - Croas ar Spernen - on a grassy bank opposite.

C Turn left here and walk along the road. After about 250m, a path goes off to the left. Ignore this unless you want a swift return to Le Relec (2.5kms away). Continue along the road, with good views on the right to the forest around Huelgoat and the quarries at Berrien.

When the road bends sharply to the left, take the track on the right. Follow this ahead for about 500m.

Note – for a quicker return to Le Relec, following the road here is another option.

D Turn left at a well-marked junction, and where the path forks soon after, take the right-hand fork. Continue ahead on the narrow path, which goes up over a gentle shoulder and then downhill. Keep straight ahead.

The path widens into a farm track with trees on both sides.

At the road, turn left along it and then round a bend to the right, before descending to a junction with the D111. Turn left here and the abbey and car-park are just ahead.

Length 8kms	**Time** 2½hrs	**Level** 2

Location & parking: SAINT MÉEN, on the D32 near Lesneven. There is a car-park directly off the main road in the village.

Refreshments: bar/restaurant at the starting point.

This is a pleasant countryside route around Saint Méen. The simple beauty of wooded valleys, little streams, gentle farmland and quiet hamlets is the most remarkable feature of the walk, and the sound of birdsong along the way more than makes up for the occasional rumble of fighter jets. In or after bad weather, some of the paths and tracks can be very muddy.

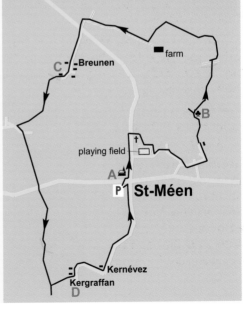

DIRECTIONS

A **Cross the road from the car-park to the church.**

The church was virtually rebuilt in 1837-8. A 16th century calvary (stone cross) which once stood in the market place is now in the cemetery.

Take the road to the right of the church for about 300m (past the town sign) to another stone cross. Turn right just beyond it.

Churchyard wall

Follow this path along the edge of a field and then bear left along a track at the end. Follow this round past the playing field and then bear left along the road. At a fork bear right and then turn left at the next junction.

Go straight ahead, past a vehicle no-entry sign, and continue to a narrow path between high banks to the left of a house. About 50m along here, bear left onto a narrow footpath.

B At a clearing where there is a junction of paths, bear left around the trees and continue ahead on the same narrow path. Bear left on the edge of a field and continue ahead.

The path goes downhill to a little stream with a plank bridge. Go straight across the track on the other side and continue up a bank on the narrow path which soon bears right.

Keep on this woodland path, which eventually bears left uphill. At the

26

top, go ahead along the edge of a field and then right at the T-junction of paths along a farm track. Continue straight ahead on this track and at a fork bear left uphill to a road. Cross straight over and continue ahead through the hamlet of Breunen.

C At the bottom of the road, bear right along a tarmac track, past a vehicle no-entry sign. Then go straight ahead downhill between tree-lined banks.

At the stream, cross carefully on rather wobbly stones and then just follow the track uphill to a road. Turn left here and then almost immediately right down a track.

At the main D32, go straight over and on down the track. This crosses a small stream and begins to climb again. At a large junction of paths, turn left up to the hamlet of Kergraffan.

D Follow the road round to the left here and then bear right to the next hamlet of Kernevez, where the road bends sharply left. Continue on this quiet road back up to the centre of Saint Méen and the starting point.

On entering the car-park, have a look at the old stone lavoir tucked away in the corner, and just beyond it, the ancient fountain of St Méen. According to legend, its waters had the power to cure skin complaints.

St Méen was one of many Welsh monks who came to Brittany in the 6th century AD and founded religious establishments.

Length 9½kms	Time 3hrs	Level 1

Location & parking: LANRIVOARÉ, just off the D68 from St-Renan. Park by the church.

Refreshments: bar in Lanrivoaré; none on route.

This easy country route follows quiet tracks around the bourg of Lanrivoaré. The main attractions are well established paths, long views over farmland, trees and hedgerows alive with birds – a true nature walk, in other words.

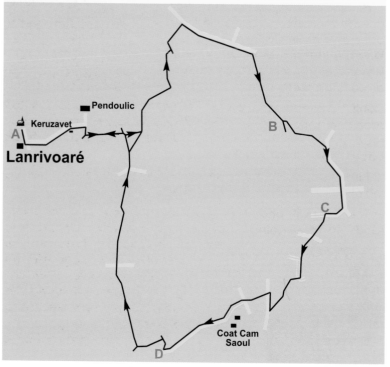

DIRECTIONS

A Walk straight up from the church towards the large sports hall and there turn left along rue de Pendoulic. Continue on this narrow road through Keruzavet and, about 120m later, turn right along a footpath opposite Pendoulic.

At a fork soon after, go left, and then at a major junction of tracks 300m later, bear right a few paces and then left (signed Kerbriec). Turn left again shortly after.

Continue ahead for about 1½kms. At the road, turn right, and then right again, 650m later, onto a footpath.

B At a fork 700m later, bear left and continue to a minor road. Turn right here and continue ahead, straight over a crossroads and then right 150m later by a grassy triangle.

C After the last house, turn left along a narrow path (ignoring the track ahead). At a small road, go straight over and continue on the path. Where it meets a stony track, bear left and then, after 150m, turn right down to a stream.

Continue ahead uphill and then turn right at the road. Turn left soon after onto another path and stay on this, crossing a minor road, for nearly a kilometre. (At Coat Cam-Saoul, the track becomes a narrow road).

D Turn right just in front of an electricity tower. Shortly after, go left at a fork and then right at the next.

Follow this path ahead for two kilometres, crossing two minor roads, and then going left at a fork, to re-join the outward route

at a major junction of footpaths. Here bear left and then left again. After 250m turn right and then left along the road back to Lanrivoaré, noting the park on the edge of the bourg as a pleasant spot for a rest.

Length 10kms	Time 3½hrs	Level 1

Location & parking: GUISSÉNY, about 8kms east of Plouguerneau on the D10 or about 10kms north of Lesneven on the D25. Park in the car-park next to the church and cemetery in the centre of the bourg.

Refreshments: in Guissény, but none on route.

A very pleasant, almost level and mainly coastal walk, this route crosses marshy land (marais) around the lake of Curnic (a good bird-watching site) on causeways before joining the coastal path. The northern coast is characterised by its fine rock formations, but there are some exceptional examples to be seen here. The directions are simple and straightforward, and the paths should not be too badly affected by wet weather.

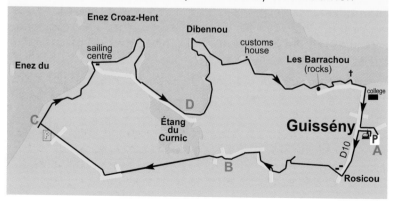

DIRECTIONS

A From the car-park, walk through the cemetery and then turn left along the cobbled road in front of the church. At the end, turn left away from the bourg along the D10.

After about 450m, in the hamlet of Rosicou, turn right by a stone cross along a tarmac road that soon becomes a narrow grassy footpath.

The path bends to the left and then continues straight ahead. At a junction of paths, bear left and follow the wider track ahead to a road.

Turn right along it (not sharp right by the no-entry sign) for about 250m and then left at the T-junction soon after.

B After about 350m, bear left at a junction and then, after about 80m, right along a straight track across the marais.

The lake (Étang du Curnic) to the right, surrounded by reeds and marshland, is a prime bird-watching area. There are observation points to the west of the lake and the causeway later in this walk is another good spot.

At the end, go ahead and then right after about 130m. Follow this road, lined with holiday chalets and cottages, to a T-junction. Go straight across, and then through a large car-park onto a sandy track to the beach.

C The coastal path crosses this path a few paces before the beach (at a gap in the fencing). Turn right along it (or alternatively, walk along the sand). The path runs along the top of the grassy dunes, with wooden fences to discourage straying from the track, which causes gradual erosion of the dunes.

Nearly all the rest of the walk is on this same coastal path. Using the map opposite may be adequate direction from now on.

At a little road near the sailing centre, turn left and follow the path round the front of the building to continue out to the grassy point. Here there are good views of the islands, Enez du and Enez Croaz-Hent, and, to the right, the lake.

Go all the way round the point and then back towards the causeway between the bay and the lake of Curnic. Keep ahead towards the start of the causeway. Turn left on a narrow tarmac track and then

after a few paces, bear left up a sandy bank onto the coastal path again, raised on a bank above the road.

D At the end of the causeway, continue on this path above the bay. Follow the path all the way through the fir trees out to the point of Dibennou. (If the tide is out, a shorter route is straight across the sandy beach). Ignore other cross paths.

The path now continues along the line of the estuary to a little stone customs house with a stepped stone roof, among large rocks.

Where the track forks here, bear left. Stay on the coastal path above the bay, ignoring other paths.

Continue ahead to the spectacular rock formations of Les Barrachou.

The path comes out onto a road just after: turn left and then left again through wooden barriers onto the path after about 60m. Continue along the coast.

The path comes out on a wide grassy space. Continue ahead and then bear left to another group of rocks and an old stone calvaire at the top of the beach. Follow the path on round to come out on the road.

Go left briefly and then turn right up towards the bourg past the large buildings of a college. Continue on this road to a junction, go straight on for about 100m, then turn left back to the church and through the cemetery to the car-park.

Length 4kms	**Time** 1½hrs	**Level** 4

Location & parking: MORLAIX. From the centre of Morlaix, use the car-park just past the viaduct.

Refreshments: cafés and restaurants on the route.

Explore this historic city by the stepped passageways (venelles) which network across the hills enclosing the city centre. As well as views over the city and its impressive viaduct, the route also passes many buildings of historical and architectural interest. Note that this walk includes many short climbs and steps of steep gradient.

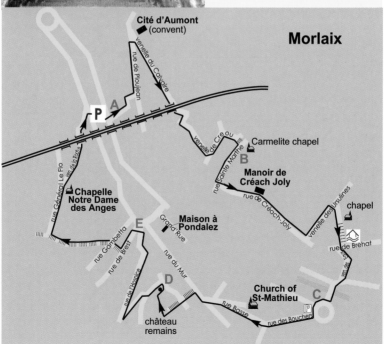

DIRECTIONS

A Facing the viaduct from the main car-park side, take the Grande venelle (now rather faded) leading up from the foot of the viaduct on the left. At the top, turn left along rue de Ploujean and then sharply back right along the venelle du Calvaire. On the left is the ancient convent, Cité Aumont, of the Calvairiennes.

Bear right along the wall for fine views over the town.

Continue ahead, under the viaduct, and then bear left uphill, follow the path round and bear left past the houses. At a T-junction turn left uphill and where the path forks go right (venelle de Creou). Where the path bends left, go straight ahead to the Carmelite chapel (15th century) and fountain.

B Go back down past the high convent walls on the rue Sainte Marthe and turn left into rue de Créach-Joly, where there is an ancient house with an old stone gateway, the Manoir de Créach-Joly, on the left.

Turn left along the venelle des Ursulines and right to the chapel, then on down the steps to the fountain. Cross the rue de Brehat and take the venelle des Eaux, its narrow entrance tucked away in a corner on the left.

C At the main road, bear right and then cross the Place Traoulen. Through a small car-park, take the rue des Bouchers ahead.

At the traffic lights, bear right along the rue Basse (note the old houses) to the church of St-Mathieu.

The present church is early 19th century, but it still has a tower from 1548, with a finely wrought iron grill (1664) at the base. The attractive interior, with its barrel-vaulted ceiling, has an interesting collection of statuary, including the famous opening statue of the virgin, Notre-Dame du Mur, which may be as early as 1400.

Continue straight ahead from the church and then bear right along the rue du Mur. After about 100m take the steps on the left. At the top, cross the narrow road and go up the steps to a grassy mound and the ruins of the château.

D Leave by the gate below the little ruined tower and turn left along the road. After 40m, take the venelle du Château on the right.

Turn right at the bottom along the rue de l'Hospice, where the walls of the old ville close can be seen on the right near the end and the Queffleuth flows on the left.

E Continue to the main road and turn sharp left into rue de Brest, cross the road and go up steps (venelle St Laurent) just past the Post Office. Cross the rue Gambetta and go up the steps of the rue Cent Marches to the left.

Just before the last flight of steps, turn right along rue Général le Flo to the Chapelle Notre-Dame des Anges on the right (a good viewpoint) and then fork right down the venelle de la Roche to return to the Place Cornic by the viaduct.

Morlaix has a long, eventful past and interesting commercial development over the centuries. The exceptional Maison à Pondalez in Grand'Rue, a narrow cobbled street in the centre of the town, is well worth a visit to discover more.

Length 5kms	**Time** 1½hrs	**Level** 2

Location & parking: LANDIVISIAU (outskirts). From the centre, take rue Louis Pasteur (direction Morlaix/Casino supermarket) then turn right at the roundabout onto the D69. Take the first exit shortly after, go left at the end of the slip-road, under the bridge and ahead for 500m towards the nursery. There is a parking area on the left opposite it.

Refreshments: cafés and restaurants in Landivisiau; none on route.

This is an easy walk through the woods of Coat Meur, mostly on well-made tracks. The area is popular for weekend outings, but otherwise usually quiet and peaceful. The route includes the Fontaine de Ste-Anasthasie in its charming setting and the lively little river Quillivaron.

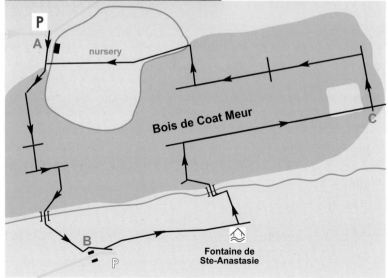

Bois de Coat Meur

nursery

Fontaine de
Ste-Anastasie

DIRECTIONS

A **From the car-park, cross the road and turn right in front of the nursery. Past the house, follow the road straight ahead between banks and then on past the plantation area on a track, which then narrows and descends. At a crossroads, go ahead downhill. At the bottom, turn left. After 150m turn right by a post and follow this down to the bridge over the Quillivaron river.**

This river valley was a centre of the leather-working industry in the 19th century, with many tanneries. An example of one from here can be seen at the Moulins de Keroat, an eco-museum near Commana.

B **Follow the path up to a hamlet, but turn left before the first house (to Fontaine Ste-Anasthasie). When the path forks, bear left downhill to the fountain.**

The pretty fountain has an inscribed date of 1803, and it was restored in 1993. There are well-used niches for offerings of flowers, and a statue of the saint overlooks the spring. There are seats here for a rest or a picnic.

Just past the fountain, turn left between two wooden barriers, signed Sentier de Coat-Meur/Ste-Anasthasie. Follow this path over the little river, then up wooden steps and bear left. Then turn right by the wooden sign. This path goes up gently among pine trees. At the next junction, turn right. Continue for a kilometre, ignoring paths off, and finally skirting a large field.

C **At the next junction, turn left uphill. Take the next turn on the left by a wooden board. At a crossroads of paths, go straight ahead. Turn right uphill at the next crossroads by a wooden fingerpost.**

Out of the trees at the top of the hill, turn left and continue for 600m, initially along the edge of the nursery, then across it. Turn right at a T-junction, back down to the small road past the nursery and the starting point.

Length 2½kms	Time 1½hrs	Level 1

Location & parking: LANDERNEAU. Use the riverside car-park (paying) in the town centre.

Refreshments: plenty of cafés and restaurants on the route.

Landerneau is an attractive estuary town with a fascinating history. Situated on the boundary of the old territories of Leon and Cornouaille, it narrowly lost out to Quimper to become the centre of administration for Finistère after the French Revolution. The sea tide reaches as far as the exceptional Pont de Rohan in the town centre, where the Élorn river flows down to join it. Landerneau was once a thriving port handling material for Brest's naval shipyards and textiles for lucrative foreign trade, and its fine town houses date from an era of maritime and commercial prosperity. This walk, based on the TO's open-air museum, reveals a wealth of architectural detail and historic interest.

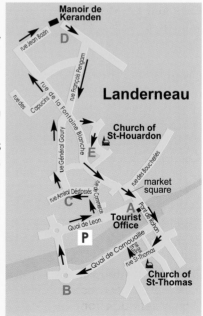

DIRECTIONS

A Start outside the tourist office, where a plaque on the wall gives information about the remarkable bridge.

The stone with gothic lettering displayed here describes how the present structure - the Pont de Rohan - was built in 1510 by Jehan II, Count of Rohan.

Walk over the bridge, stopping at the crêperie on the right.

This is the Maison Gillart (1639), in yellow stone from Logonna (to the west) in renaissance style. High on the south wall is a sundial decorated by two lions.

Just over the bridge on the right, another plaque marks the site of the hospital founded in 1336.

The ground floor retains its handsome logonna stone. Note the figurine above.

Continue ahead over the bridge for about 80m, then turn right in front of a fountain, along the rue St-Thomas.

No 5, the auberge Notre-Dame de Rumengol, dates from 1668. At the back of the house, look up to see the latrine 'extension'.

Opposite, at No 6, is a 'Maison à encorbellement', which once had a jutting wooden façade, now slate-covered.

Continue ahead between the two buildings to a little square with the church of St-Thomas on the left.

Dedicated to Thomas Becket, Archbishop of Canterbury, this church is first mentioned in the 13th century, but was rebuilt later.

Opposite the church is the ossuary of St-Cadou (1635), for the remains of the dead. Above the plaque is a death's head and crossed bones. During the Revolution, the building was used as a workshop for making soldiers' boots and later a chimney was added when it became the sacristan's lodging.

Across the square is the Auberge of the 13 Moons.

This 16th century house provided a meeting place for the 'Club des amis de la Revolution'. Traces of the moons are just visible on the façade.

Take the rue aux Fruits at the side of the Auberge down to the river, then turn left and walk along the Quai de Cornouaille. The Ancient Priory of St-Thomas is on the left, slightly set back from the road.

This 16th century building was a dependence of the Abbey at nearby Daoulas.

B Turn right over the bridge, then right back towards the town along the Quai de Léon. Cross over after about 80m.

At No. 26 two huge chimneys top the Hotel d'Armateur (1725)- now a dental practice! The lucarne windows with their granite surrounds at the top of the house, are flanked by two 'false eyes'. Next door is a smaller house from 1626, with a 'pot a feu' design typical of the period.

Continue and turn left up the rue de Commerce. On the left, at No.5, is the Maison Duthoya.

This striking house(1667) was owned by the Duthoya family, 17th century ship-owners and mayors of the town.

Continue ahead to the Auberge le Réveil Matin.

The auberge retains its medieval character. Note the two elaborate gargoyles. The eastern side is faced with local schist.

A few metres to the right of the auberge is the Maison à la Sirène at No. 14.

Here the ancient carved figure of a siren can still be seen on high.

Continue up to the right of the auberge, and then turn left into rue Amiral Desfossés.

C Turn right up the rue Général Goury and go straight over at the crossroads. When the road joins the rue de la Fontaine Blanche, turn left. The Convent of the Capucins is on the left shortly after.

This order was established in Landerneau in 1636, when this impressive building was begun. Walk down the side road to see some very interesting chimneys and an ancient doorway.

Continue up the street past the convent and turn right along the rue Jehan Bazin (historian, 1901-1981), where there are some lovely houses. At the end, in a little park, is a very attractive manor house.

The Manoir de Keranden retains only a stair-turret and a ruined wall from its 17th century origins. The current facade was remodelled in renaissance style in 1904.

D Continue on through the park and down to the main road. Turn right down the rue François Pengam. After 150m, there is a former convent on the left.

The Convent of the Ursulines was housed in this very elaborate building, in horseshoe shape, with an impressive arcade.

Continue ahead, then bear left and follow the road round to the church of St-Houardon.

The church was rebuilt in 1858 and restored in 1957. Remains of the 16th century original are found in the gargoyles.

E From the plaque, turn back into a pretty little square, where the Presbytery of St-Houardon is on the opposite side at No 29. Turn left and continue downhill into a pedestrian only area.

Note No. 10, the Hotel Particulier, an 18th century building, with a fine porch and a wrought-iron balcony. It was built in 1760 and used as the College de la ville from 1836-1890. The elaborate granite house at No. 4 was the seat of the marechaussée(a sort of 17th century police official). An empty niche marks where a coat-of-arms was once displayed.

At the little market square, go left along the rue des Boucheries for a short way.

No. 6 is a former 16th century logis, with a roof-level carving of a female figure at one end and a male carrying a pichet at the other.

Return to the market square where the finest building of all is the last on this tour.

The Maison de la Sénéchaussée (also often called the Maison de la Duchesse Anne) was built in 1664. The north face with its three over-lapping storeys, is of wood covered by well-patterned slates. A beautiful building from any angle!

Leave the market square and cross the main road to the starting point.

Length 5½kms	Time 1½hrs	Level 1

Location & parking: LAMPAUL-PLOUDALMÉZEAU, 2kms north of Ploudalmézeau, which is on the D26 from Brest.
Drive straight through the village, past the mairie, towards the sea. At the bottom of the road, turn right towards the municipal camping and then immediately left to the car-park by the dunes.

Refreshments: bar in the village.

The delightful bay here is dotted with rocky islands.
This gentle stroll takes in some quiet country tracks with sea views, and a Neolithic alley grave among the grassy dunes before returning along the sandy beach,
where swimming is possible.

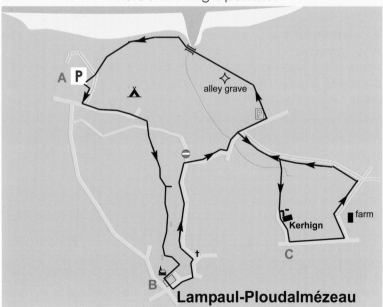

Lampaul-Ploudalmézeau

DIRECTIONS

A From the entrance to the parking, turn left and continue ahead into the camping. Turn right after the children's play area, cross the narrow road and take the track ahead up towards the village. Where the track forks, bear right. Pass two stone lavoirs and come out by the church.

The 17th century church was damaged by lightning and almost entirely rebuilt in 1856, retaining the earlier north porch.

B Go into the churchyard and then through the cemetery. At the gates, turn left down the road.

An early stone pillar (stele) is immediately to the right on the corner outside the cemetery.

Follow the road to a stone cross and then bear left down the route du Ribl. At the bottom, follow it round to the right (no-entry sign straight ahead). At a T-junction, turn left.

After about 120m, turn right up a stony track. Ignore grassy tracks on the right until, after about 150m, turn right past a wooden post down towards a stream. Continue ahead towards the houses of Kerhign.

On the left is an impressive manor house with a turret staircase on the back and a fine arched front door.

C At the T-junction turn left and continue ahead for 250m, down into a dip. As the road starts to climb, turn left towards a farm. Follow the road to the left of the farm and ahead when it becomes a track.

After 300m, turn left towards the sea. This track between fields has excellent views of the bay. Follow this all the way back to the road. Turn right and left shortly after into a little car-park. The path across the dunes to the alley grave is marked by a fingerpost. Continue ahead to the next post and then bear left.

This gallery tomb (allée couverte du Ribyl) dates from about 3000BC. Neolithic and Bronze Age finds were made on excavation in the 1920s. These are illustrated on an information board nearby.

From the alley grave, cross the dunes towards the beach and bear left. A wooden bridge spans the creek of the Ribl. After that, walk along the dunes or the sand, back to the car-park (about 500m).

ADDITIONAL SUGGESTIONS
for walking in North Finistère

Here are some more good places to follow marked circuits or just to park and walk.

POUL RODOU – Turn left off the D64 along the coast just before Locquirec and park near the viewing table or the café at Poul Rodou. There is excellent coastal path walking here.

BARNÉNEZ – Past the famous cairn, turn left down to the coast path for superb views of the Bay of Morlaix and the Château du Taureau, a fortified island. For a longer walk, it is possible to cross the narrow neck of the peninsula and return up the east coast.

ROSCOFF – This lovely old town is well worth a visit for its own sake, regardless of the ferry port just outside. The promenade and harbour area are excellent places for a relaxing stroll, and from here there are two marked longer circuits: the 2hr Circuit des Fontaines and the 1½hr Circuit de l'Aber.

GUERLESQUIN – There is a walking circuit around lakes in the valley of the river Guic on the edge of this petite cité de caractère .

LANDES du CRAGOU – Just off the D769, past the hamlet of Penmergues, near the Croix-courte, is a nature reserve with walking trails by this striking range of wild hills.

LE RELEC – From the car-park by the ancient abbey church there is a short walking circuit through the woods, over streams and past an old fontaine, returning to the village alongside its pretty lake. (NB: for a longer walk here, see p. 22)

BAY OF KERNIC – For a different aspect of the coastal path, walk from the point at Porz Meur inland along the Bay of Kernic (about 1km) to the half-submerged Neolithic alley grave on the beach.

PLAGE de KEREMMA – Off the D10 between Goulven and Plouescat is this fantastic beach with acres of sand and dunes. The Maison des Dunes has information about nature trails in the area.

MÉNÉHAM – The beach and rocky coast here are both very attractive, but the addition of an eerie deserted fishing village provides an unusual extra dimension. There is a marked 8km circuit from here, starting inland towards Théven and a series of other hamlets before returning along the coastal path.

LA MARTYRE is justly famous for its parish close, but there are also various walking circuits here, with good long views. The Circuit de la Haie is 5½kms.

ABER WRAC'H – There is fine walking on the coastal path west

of this harbour village to the vast Baie des Anges (2x3kms), or in the other direction to the Pont du Paluden (2x5kms). These are worthy linear walks with good views either way, but both have alternative return routes inland if preferred.

PLOUVIEN has a 10km rural circuit starting from the place des Fusillés, including the valley of the Aber Benoit.

BREST – On the eastern edge of the city, just off the N165, the area around the Conservatoire Botanique (outstanding botanical gardens with many endangered species) provides plenty of pleasant walking in a landscaped park with a series of lakes.

SAINT-RENAN – Here there is a marked 11km circuit around the lakes which now occupy former sites of the pewter industry. The town itself also has much of historic and architectural interest.

POINTE de ST-MATHIEU – The dramatic coastline here provides fantastic views, with a ruined abbey, lighthouses and striking rock formations. For a 9km circuit, follow the coastpath east for about 3½kms, then turn inland to Trémeur and return through a series of hamlets to the coast to retrace the route for the last kilometre.

Centre	13 HUELGOAT	Long
Length 12kms	**Time** 4hrs	**Level** 3

Location & parking: HUELGOAT. Park in the car-park near the mairie, behind the church in the main square.

Refreshments: cafés, crêperies and restaurants in Huelgoat.

This is a memorable walk through the depths of a peaceful and atmospheric forest. First following a canal out to the old mining areas, the route then returns along the River Argent, with its extraordinary granite boulders of remarkable sizes and shapes, before crossing the D769 to explore the Wild Boars' Pool and an Iron Age camp. At the end is the famous granite 'Chaos' on the edge of the lakeside town of Huelgoat.

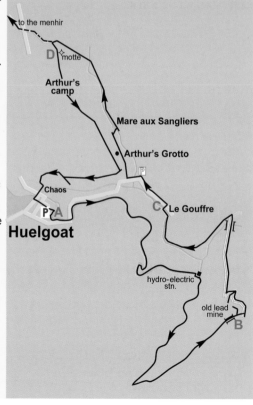

DIRECTIONS

A **From the car-park, follow the footpath sign down to the canal, cross a bridge and turn right along the bank. Follow this to steps up to a main road. Cross the road and turn left. After a few metres, the canal path sign is on the bank on the right.**

Follow the canal, on the left bank, for 4kms through the forest, (ignoring other paths) until a metal bridge by a small hydro-electric station. Cross this and turn left to a clearing. Then bear right alongside a dry canal bed, and follow it round the head of the valley for 2kms.

B **Towards the end of the canal, cross a wooden bridge over a gully and follow the path ahead. To reach the mine site, either go first left down a steep path or, for an easier descent, go ahead to a T-junction of tracks and turn left, then very sharp left at the next junction into the site.**

This area was first mined for lead and silver by the Celts and Romans, but had its heyday in the 18th-19th centuries. The lake in Huelgoat and two canals (1761 and 1772-4) were constructed by German workers to run the hydraulic machinery needed for efficient exploitation. The old mine workings, wheel and ruined master's house remain today.

From the ruined house, return to the junction of paths and go sharp left downhill, continuing ahead at the bottom along the stony road. (There are information boards about the mines to the left here).

Continue to a bridge over the river. Cross it and follow the footpath sign to the left. After about a kilometre, the path reaches the riverbank. Continue up to the Gouffre.

At the Gouffre a torrent of water crashes down the deep gorge. Here, in legend, Dahut, daughter of King Gradlon, lured her many lovers to their deaths. Their cries are still heard echoing from the depths...

The belvedere, a short steep climb above the gouffre, is on an 11th century defensive motte. There is also a memorial to the poet Victor Ségalen.

C At the Gouffre, go up stone steps to the main road, turn left and continue for about 300m where there is a large parking area and hut on the other side of the road. Cross, but then continue on the road for a little way to a path on the right (to Arthur's Grotto). Go straight up here past the grotto and then fork right down to the Mare aux Sangliers (Wild Boars' Pool).

Cross the bridge and go up steps to a T-junction of paths. Turn left and follow this path all the way (about 1km) to an old stone slab bridge (Pont Gwen), then cross this to bear left uphill on a narrow path between high banks. The path ends in a glade at the entrance to Arthur's Camp.

DETOUR (2x850m): to see the menhir (huge standing stone) at Kerampeulven, take the small road to the right to a main road. Cross straight over and continue to the pretty hamlet where the menhir is on the left after a few houses. Return to the glade by Arthur's camp.

Arthur's camp is actually an Iron Age hill fort from about the 1st century BC, possibly a tribal settlement of the Osismes. It contained a sizable community – evidence of enclosures and hearths - with an inner defensive area. Roman coins found here may indicate that Caesar's conquering armies took over the camp at some point. The motte at the entrance is a 10th century defensive work.

D Enter the camp past the motte on the left and follow this broad path all the way through various sets of ramparts.

After descending the hill, turn right along the Chemin des Amoureux. Bear right at the end to the main 'Chaos' where the granite boulders are at their most spectacular.

Follow the path through these, past the Ménage de Vierge, and then bearing left down and up steps towards the Grotte du Diable, where there is a ladder down to a dark underground chamber with a torrent of water below (optional!). Continue past this through a tunnel of huge rocks to the right to come out by the lake in the town.

Cross the road and go straight ahead by the lake for a few metres. On the left before a shop is a very narrow passageway leading up to the market square. The car-park is behind the church here.

Centre	14 MONTS D'ARRÉE	Long

Length 14kms	Time 4½hrs	Level 3

Location & parking: by the reservoir of St-Michel and in the Monts d'Arrée, around the D785 between Roc'h Trévezel and Brasparts. Park at the Ferme des Artisans, directly off the D785 near Mont. St-Michel de Brasparts (hill with chapel on top, visible for miles around).

Refreshments: possibly at the Ferme des Artisans in high season, but own provisions advised.

This wonderful circuit including the peat bogs (tourbières) around the reservoir of St-Michel and the high open moorland (landes) of the Monts d'Arrée provides varied walking with excellent long views and two outstanding viewpoints on the hill-tops. The route includes uneven stony paths, several gradual climbs and a short, steep one at Mont. St-Michel. Care should be taken on the wooden walkways across the marshes in bad weather.

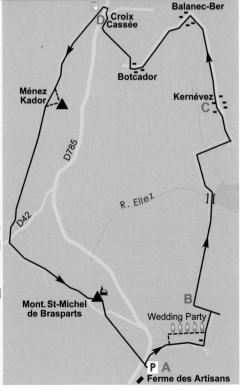

The Ferme des Artisans, in a group of attractive old stone buildings, houses an art gallery and a large shop on two floors selling Breton products. Open every day in high season and weekends otherwise.

DIRECTIONS

A Out of the entrance to the car-park, turn right and walk for 250m alongside the main road. At the wooden fingerpost, turn right down a track.

DETOUR: best viewed from the top of Mont. St-Michel, a megalithic alignment of small standing stones is to the left of the path here. It is often called the Wedding Party, from the legend that revelling guests were turned to stone for refusing to make way for a priest carrying the sacrament.

To walk through the stones, turn left along the top of the first field, continue to a junction of paths and go right. The last three stones are separate from the others beyond a line of pine trees. Go straight ahead past them to join the track alongside the house mentioned below. Turn left to rejoin the walk.

Turn left past a house in the trees on the left of the track. Continue ahead over the shoulder of the hill, with a wonderful view across the lake.

To the right is a former nuclear power station, the first to be built in France, and long since decommissioned.

At a T-junction of paths, turn left and continue past a row of fir trees for about 150m to a junction of paths over a plank 'bridge'.

B Turn right here and follow the very narrow path through the heather and then over the wooden walkways towards the lake. KEEP TO THE PATH here.

The bleak marshland surrounding the reservoir is known in legend as Yeun Ellez, the place where the entrance to the Celtic underworld was situated. Here nocturnal washer-women seek the help of unwary passers-by to carry their baskets, only to ensnare them in their coils of death before the sun comes up...

Cross a bridge over the Ellez and continue ahead. Bear right over a stream, and at a junction of paths, turn left to Kernévez.

Walk right through the hamlet and continue along the road to Balanec-Ber. In this settlement turn left towards Botcador, nearly 1 kilometre ahead. Go through this hamlet and turn right along a track after the last house. Follow this path (NB: stream-bed in places) all the way up to Croix Cassée by the main D785.

C Turn right along the main road for a few metres and then cross to a track and parking area at the foot of Ménez Kador.

Take the track to the left up to the summit (380m) and a very short detour to the rocks.

From the rocks, return to the track and continue over the brow of the hill, heading towards some radio masts behind fir trees ahead. Bear left through the trees and to the D42. Turn right briefly and then left up the track to the top of Mont. St-Michel.

Up to Ménez Kador

This hill has long pagan associations with the sun god. The chapel of St-Michel was placed here by Christians to usurp the place of earlier celtic worship (like Glastonbury Tor).

From the summit, the car-park by the Ferme des Artisans is visible. Take the most direct path down from the hill (If visibility is poor just follow the little road) and cross the main road with care.

Centre	15 TAL-AR-GROAZ	Long

Length 12kms	Time 4hrs	Level 4

Location & parking: TAL-AR-GROAZ, Crozon peninsula. From the roundabout here take the D887 towards Crozon, but turn off left almost immediately to the ruined Chapelle St-Laurent and park nearby.

Refreshments: none on route.

This is a varied walk, including the ups and downs of the coastal path, with one very steep climb. In addition to wonderful views of the Aber, there are sandy beaches, dramatic headlands and some pretty tree-lined country footpaths. Historical points of note include a small group of standing stones and a huge old lime kiln.

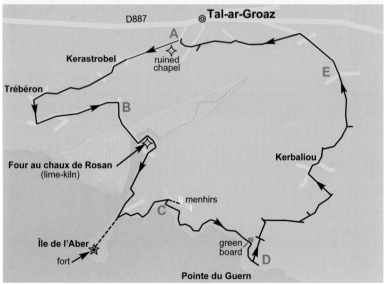

DIRECTIONS

A **Take the track past the ruined chapel to the next hamlet of Kerastrobel. Where the track ends, go ahead on the road and bear left at the next fork. At a crossroads, go straight ahead on a track. At the end, bear left towards the houses in the hamlet of Trébéron. At the end of the road, turn left.**

(There is an ancient lavoir just round the corner to the right here).

At a T-junction, turn left along a road above the water (or marshes if the tide is out). Ignore the road to the right 250m later, and continue to a T-junction.

B **Here turn right downhill to the causeway across the aber. Turn left after 300m at a sign for Four au Chaux de Rosan.**

A path at the side of this old lime kiln leads up to the top of the shaft and gives some excellent views up and down the aber. These will vary enormously according to the state of the tide, but wildlife will be equally interesting regardless.

Continue on the main path round the kiln and then turn right back to the road. Cross straight over here and follow the coastal path along the rocky shore, with red-coloured cliffs to the left and the river-bed to the right.

NOTE: if the tide is high it will be necessary to take the grassy path above, still following the coast.

Either way, after about 800m there is a causeway out to the Île de l'Aber.

DETOUR (2x750m): if the tide permits, it is possible to go out to the end of the 'île'. The fort here was built in 1862, and consists of barracks with an artillery platform above.

To continue the walk turn left up over the rocks onto a track and then bear right before the road onto the narrow coastal path. This comes out by a stony track.

DETOUR (2x250m): just ahead on the track at this point are two Neolithic standing stones (menhirs) on the left and a third further on to the right.

C To continue the walk, turn sharp right down towards the beach. Follow the coastal path along above it (there are ways down to the sand if required), up some steps and then on along the cliffs, keeping to the right or straight on at any path junctions.

After about 800m, aim for a green board at the foot of the promontory ahead. Follow the path past this and then turn up left through the trees soon after. This short section up onto the shoulder of the Pointe du Guern is very steep indeed.

D Once up, turn left, inland, on a narrow grassy track.

At a junction of paths, go straight on. At the next, bear left and right again immediately. At a fork, bear left. Ignore the next track to the left and continue ahead for about 300m to a finger-post. Turn left here, down to the hamlet of Kerbaliou.

Turn right at the road and go straight ahead at a junction immediately after. Continue until the road bears right and there go left on a concreted track, and then right soon after.

After a while this narrows to a pleasant, leafy footpath. Where the path divides, bear left.

E After about 650m, go straight over at a small road and continue up a tarmac road. At the next crossroads, go straight over and then turn left along a track about 120m after.

When this finally comes out on a small road, turn right and continue uphill until a grassy track goes off to the left.

Where the path opens out and forks, bear right. At the road go straight across. This road bears right and ahead are the fingerposts at the start of the walk near the ruined chapel.

Centre	16 MÉNEZ HOM	Long

Length 13½kms	Time 4½hrs	Level 3

Location & parking: around MÉNEZ HOM. On the D887, 12kms west of Châteaulin, towards Crozon, Use the car-park opposite the Church of Ste-Marie du Ménez Hom.

Refreshments: none on route.

The best views in Finistère are to be had from the top of Ménez Hom, weather permitting. This walk climbs steadily through woods to the summit and then down to the coastal plain, skirting the round hill called Hielc'h. Points of interest include a sacred spring and a Neolithic burial chamber, but the most abiding memory of this route is the views. If possible, choose a clear day!

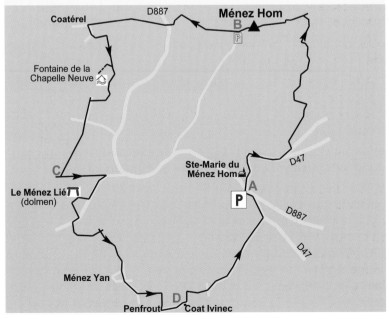

DIRECTIONS

A **From the parking, cross the main D887 and walk down the D47 opposite for about 800m before taking a minor road on the left (signed Kergaoc). After about 200m, turn left up a narrow track.**

This meanders through the trees for about 1½ kms, gradually climbing the shoulder of Ménez Hom. Once out of the trees, there are views of the sea behind.

Continue up to a wooden marker post and turn left up onto the summit. The Rade de Brest gradually comes into view ahead and the suspension bridge, Pont de Térénez, over the Aulne estuary.

When another path comes in from the left, bear right uphill. There is a viewing table at the top.

And the views will be stunning in clear weather. Inland are the Monts d'Arrée to the north and the Black Mountains to the

south; seawards the Cap-Sizun peninsula, culminating in the Pointe du Van and the Pointe du Raz is to the left and Cap de la Chèvre at the end of the Crozon peninsula to the right.

Ménez Hom was once a pagan site of sun-worship, and a statue of the celtic goddess Brigit was found here. It is also the legendary burial place of King Marc'h, who used to conceal his horse's ears under a hat.

B **From the viewing table continue straight ahead (ignoring the path to the car-park on the left) on a grassy path directly towards the sea and continue down to the main road visible below. This descent is quite steep and needs care. Keep straight ahead. When the path comes out into a field, turn left to the road and cross it, continuing ahead down a green lane directly opposite.**

In the hamlet of Coatérel, turn sharp left at the first junction. On the next bend take the track to the left, signed Fontaine de la Chapelle Neuve. To see this, turn right after about 600m.

DETOUR (2x150m): The waters of the fontaine were said to have miraculous powers of curing lameness in children. After bathing her child, the mother would place it on the stone nearby, sit on the steps of the calvary herself and call the child to walk to her.

Continue on the main path uphill, bearing right towards the top. Turn left along a road with good views. At the crossroads, go straight across and continue ahead on a stony track.

C At the next junction, turn left and then at the road (D108), turn sharp right down it for about 300m.

A Neolithic dolmen is visible across the field on the right.

By the trees (marker on trunk), turn right towards the dolmen and then along the edge of a field. At the dolmen, bear left along the edge of the next field to two wooden posts. Turn left between them back to the road. Turn right for about 150m and then take the track on the left.

Follow this stony track which soon bears left and uphill. After about 300m, take the track on the right, which drops down into the hamlet of Ménez Yan. Go straight through on the same road.

About 200m after the crossroads, turn left along a straight grassy track. Stay on this, bearing right down to the hamlet of Penfrout. Turn left along the small tarmac road just before the farm buildings.

D Continue ahead to Coat Ivinec and turn left just past the little house. Follow the path round to the right and on to the road. Ignore the immediate left turn, cross the open space and then bear left uphill along a minor road for about 1km. As the road climbs, there are excellent views across to the Black Mountains on the right.

At the next junction, turn left along the D47. The car-park is about 250m ahead.

Centre	17 MÉNEZ MEUR	Medium
Length 7½kms	**Time** 2½hrs	**Level** 3

Location & parking: MÉNEZ MEUR, on the D342, south from Sizun. Park in the large car-park at Ménez Meur.

Refreshments: at start and finish in season only.

NOTE: this circuit is available during the opening hours of the nature reserve at Ménez Meur and an entrance ticket (good value) must be purchased. The reserve is open every day May to September; Wednesday and Sunday afternoons in March, April, October and November; school holidays only (afternoons) in winter.

This circuit is included here, despite the minor limitations noted above, because of the excellent range of countryside and fine views it offers. The walk starts in the nature reserve where many Breton breeds of domestic animals (as well as deer, wolves and wild boar) can be seen and then tracks through dense pine woods, open marshy land and green lanes to various fine rocky viewpoints before returning to the park. Care is needed on some of the paths in bad weather.

DIRECTIONS

A From the ticket office, turn right and follow the marked trail (orange slash) to a look-out post reached by wooden steps. This overlooks the deer enclosure and also has good long views. Continue down more steps, and then follow the orange symbols past the deer, pigs and goats. Turn left (NB: orange symbol) to leave the animal park on a long green track.

B After about 300m, turn right through a sombre pine wood and follow the path to a T-junction with finger-posts.

Turn right for a very short distance to the Belvedere, an outcrop of schist, with fantastic views over the Monts d'Arrée, closer countryside and the town of Sizun. Then return to the marked circuit and follow the path again to another mini-diversion. It is well worth taking a few paces to the left here to see the Abri de Carrier (quarryman's shelter) built of schist, with a branch and turf roof. Return to the marked route.

The path now descends through the pines. At a junction there is the choice of a short-cut for this circuit to the left, but go right for the main trail which runs along below the Belvedere. A tiny plank bridge crosses the outlet from a schist-lined fontaine shortly before the ruins of an old farmhouse, one eerie wall still standing.

C Turn left immediately before this and go ahead through the trees. Go left along a most attractive wide tree-lined track and then left again at the end. Here the track is open and can be very boggy in wet weather.

D Follow markers at the end to the right and right again immediately. This narrow path borders a stream and then crosses marshland on wooden boards. Bear right at the very end out of the trees to a narrow road.

E Here, either follow the sign to the right towards the hamlet of Balanec Huella and then left to the rocky viewpoint on Roc'h an Daol ahead and round in a circle back to this point, or go straight up the road, bear right at the finger-post (Circuit Roc'h an Daol) and then turn right

after 175m up to the summit on a narrow path and then return to this point by the same route.

On return, continue ahead down the narrow road for about 800m to a crossroads of paths and turn right along a wide brackish track to skirt around Roc'h Luz. Follow the path ahead, which eventually narrows alongside an animal enclosure, until it turns left into the park again (wild boar enclosure to the right).

From here, continue straight ahead for the most direct route to the refreshments (in season) and exit, or follow the signs to the right on a short detour past the wolves first.

Length 10kms	**Time** 3hrs	**Level** 2

Location & parking: LOQUEFFRET on the D14, west from Huelgoat. Park by the mairie and church in the centre.

Refreshments: bar in Loqueffret, café in St-Herbot.

This fine country walk, along a good variety of paths, has many splendid views across the hilly landscape of central Finistère. It is also a peaceful route through sparsely populated terrain, but includes the attractive village of St-Herbot with its outstanding church. The last stretch crosses the wild spaces of the 'landes' or heathland typical of the Monts d'Arrée. In wet weather, some sections will be difficult, but not impassable.

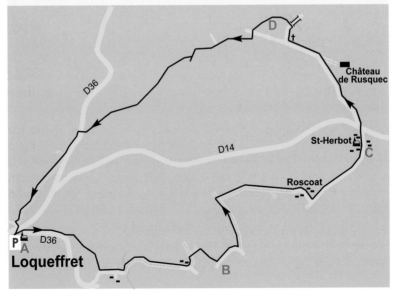

DIRECTIONS

A From the car-park, go towards and then to the left of the church and then turn right down the D36. After 400m, where the road bends right, turn left along a track and continue ahead between banks. (This may be a muddy start in poor conditions). Go straight ahead at a junction of paths.

At the road, turn left and continue ahead past a hamlet on the right.

Turn left 150m later, before a stream, and stay on this track all the way to the next hamlet. Here follow the road and go left when it forks. Continue uphill, and turn right shortly after along the edge of a field.

When the track goes left uphill, go straight on and then right immediately, downhill on a narrow path between hedges.

B Turn left at the road and continue ahead until the road bends right and there turn left uphill on a track. After about 450m, turn right before the crest of the hill. Go straight on at a junction and follow this track downhill to the hamlet of Roscoat.

Follow the road round to the right and down to a T-junction. Turn left and walk along the road to St-Herbot.

The early 16th century church of St-Herbot has a fine oak screen in the chancel and stone tables for offerings, such as hair from cows' tails, to the patron saint of cattle. The simple but powerfully expressive calvary outside is from 1571.

C Continue straight through the village, past the church and up to the main road. Bear left past the telephone box and cross the D14 to continue ahead up a minor road opposite, signed Barrage de St-Herbot.

Stay on this road uphill for just over a kilometre, passing the entrance to the (private) 15th century Château de Rusquec. Turn right 300m later, just after a stone cross.

After about 200m, turn sharp left before the bridge along a narrow path.

It is worth just going ahead to the bridge, which spans the Ellez. This river flows across the often mist-covered central basin below the Monts d'Arrée. Its surrounding marshland (tourbières) is the scene for many Breton legends. (See Walk 14).

The Ellez

D Follow this, which soon bends to the left, to a little road. Go straight over and follow the track round to the right. Where a road comes up from the right, go straight on. Soon after, where the path bends left and forks, go right.

The long low hill of Ménez Du is to the left, and there are superb long views to the right to the Monts d'Arrée, including the chapel on top of Mont. St-Michel de Brasparts. The now defunct nuclear power station at Brennilis is also visible.

Stay on this path, ignoring right turns, for just over a kilometre to the main road (D36). Here cross, turn left and walk with care along the road for about 200m, before going off right, but parallel with the road (fingerpost to Loqueffret).

Follow this track back to the bourg and turn left to come out opposite the mairie and the starting point.

Centre	19 CHÂTEAUNEUF-du-FAOU	Medium

Length 8½kms	Time 2½hrs	Level 2

Location & parking: CHÂTEAUNEUF-du-FAOU. From the town centre, follow the D36 (direction Rosporden) and immediately across the river, turn right (road leading to Centre de Vacances) and stop in any of the parking areas.

Refreshments: In Châteauneuf, but none on route.

Châteauneuf-du-Faou

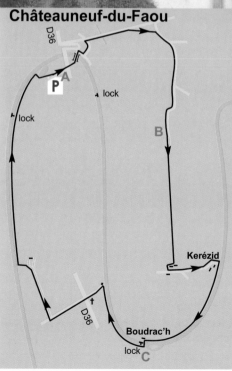

This is a scenic walk in the environs of the attractive little town of Châteauneuf-du-Faou. The route starts at an ancient bridge, then passes through quiet hamlets to the beautiful Aulne River, part of the old Nantes/Brest canal, complete with locks, at this point in its tortuous course. There are also fine views of the château of Trévarez in the Black Mountains.

DIRECTIONS

A Cross the D36 and, a few paces to the left, go down the stone steps by a wooden fingerpost. Cross the old bridge ahead.

The Pont du Roy dates from the 17th century.

Across the bridge, turn right and then after about 175m, turn left past the bar/restaurant (Le Chaland) up the rue des Peupliers. Continue up to a T-junction and then turn right along an old Roman road.

Follow this ahead as it dips to cross a stream and then, about 200m up the slope, take a narrow earth footpath between hedges to the right.

Ignore a path coming in from the right. Go straight ahead to a road and turn right along it.

Follow the road round to the right, ignoring a left fork, and continue straight ahead. Over the rise, where the road forks, bear right.

B Continue straight ahead when the road eventually turns into a track.

From here there are views across the Aulne to the Black Mountains and the 'château rose' of Trévarez on the wooded slopes. The château, built at the end of the 19th century, is open to the public. Although only a few rooms of the house can be seen, Trévarez is justly famous for its gardens.

At the end, the track bears right and left past old farm buildings and meets a narrow road. Go left along it and left at the next fork (direction Kerézid). Stay on this little road all the way to the canal.

The ruined (at the time of writing) house on the right at the roadside at Kerézid has a date-stone of 1586, visible to the left of the arched opening at first floor level.

At the canal, turn right and follow the path to the next lock at Boudrac'h.

C Cross the canal here over a narrow footbridge and turn right down the opposite bank.

The lock at Boudrac'h

The Nantes-Brest canal (360kms long, with 237 locks) was conceived as a military project, to secure an internal supply-line to Brest, but in the event its main traffic was commercial. The construction began in 1811 and was completed in 1836. Its main focus now is leisure activities.

After about 500m, turn sharp left by a small stone house and follow this road uphill to a junction with the main road by a stone cross.

Cross the D36 and go ahead down a narrow road (direction Stéraon).

After about 450m, turn sharp right along a gravel track and continue ahead. At a fork, bear left. Just before the buildings, turn left along a green path down to the river bank again.

Turn right and follow the canal path all the way back, past the Écluse Châteauneuf (lock), and, round a long bend, towards the town.

At the inland mooring lake, take a track to the right (leading to a narrow tarmac road) and follow this, with the lake to the left, back to the entrance to the Centre de Vacances and the various parking areas.

Centre	20 CAMARET	Medium
Length 9kms	**Time** 3hrs	**Level** 3

Location & parking: CAMARET, on the D8 from Crozon. At the second mini-roundabout on the edge of Camaret, go straight on to Pointe de Pen-hir (not right to centre ville). Keep straight ahead at each mini-roundabout to the end of this long road, and turn left at a T-junction. Continue ahead all the way to the point, where there is a large car-park.

Refreshments: cafés and restaurants in Camaret.

This route follows the spectacular rocky coastline from Pointe de Pen-hir to the delightful port of Camaret. It then returns through the town, via the remarkable Neolithic alignments of Lagatjar and a sheltered beach to the point. The views for most of the walk are exceptional, but note that care should be taken in walking along the stony paths on these rugged cliffs.

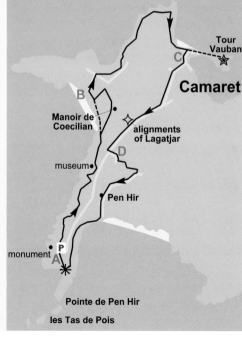

DIRECTIONS

On the cliff-top at the Pointe de Pen-hir there is a large granite memorial to the Breton resistance movement.

A From (facing) the memorial, go right along the coastal path. After about a kilometre, there is a series of German fortifications.

The Museum of the Battle of the Atlantic is housed in one of these bunkers. Its displays tell the grim story of the conflict between German U-boats and Allied navies in the second World War.

About 600m ahead, the path divides (just in front of the first of a series of large houses). Ahead is the spectacular bay of Pen Hat. Bear right here, along the fence, to the ruined house on the hill-top to the right of the path. (Or left straight down to the beach, if preferred).

The house was built in 1905 for the famous surrealist poet, St-Pol-Roux, who later called it Manoir de Coecilian, after his son of that name who died in the first world war. In 1940, a German soldier  attacked the old man and his daughter in the house, killing their servant who tried to protect them. The poet died a few months later. The ransacked house eventually fell into ruin.

Continue past the ruins and bear left down to the beach.

B Turn up the road from the car-park there and at the T-junction, cross over to rejoin the narrow earth coastal path, bearing right up the hillside.

Follow this all the way around the next point, from where the path descends to the engaging little port of Camaret. Bear left through a small park and then out onto the road by the swimming beach.

DETOUR (2x500m): Ahead is a curving jetty (sillon) at the end of which is the 17th century Tour Vauban, part of Louis XIV's defensive programme, and the Church of Notre-Dame de Rocamadour, which lost the top of its belfry during an English attack in 1694.

C Turn right and then take the next road on the right, uphill away from the harbour. Follow this for just over a kilometre to the Alignments of Lagatjar on the right of the road.

These Neolithic alignments, consisting of more than 140 stones of varying sizes, are over 5000 years old. The site was presumably used for some sort of religious rituals, on what would then have been an empty headland.

D Continue ahead for about 300m and then turn left down a small road (signed Kerbonn). Follow the road round to the right and then take a narrow path between hedges to the left shortly after.

When the path comes out on a narrow road, turn right through the hamlet of Pen Hir and then left at a fork soon after. This road leads down to the beach of Veryac'h.

Turn right here along the coastal path and follow it up along the cliffs to the very end of Pointe de Pen-hir. The distinctive line of rocks out to sea is called les Tas de Pois (the piles of peas).

Turn right to return to the parking area by the monument.

Centre	21 CARHAIX	Short

Length 6kms	Time 1½hrs	Level 1

Location & parking: CARHAIX-PLOUGUER, where the D764 enters from the west. Park by the Church of St-Trémeur.

Refreshments: in Carhaix, but only waterside picnic areas on route.

Carhaix is a town of Roman origins, with much of historical and architectural interest, especially in the area around the Church of St-Trémeur. The walk is mainly a country one, exploring the valley of the river Hyères, with some memorably lovely paths and watery scenes, in a great loop around the west of the town. There are no great changes of gradient and most of the paths are hard-surfaced, so it is a very pleasant and relaxing stroll in attractive scenery with all the benefits of the town also near at hand.

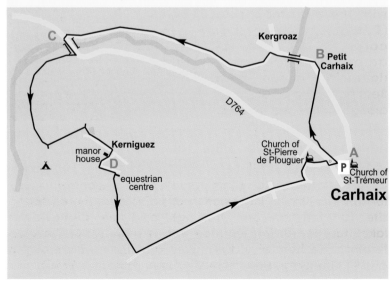

DIRECTIONS

A From the corner of the church car-park by the mini-roundabout, go straight ahead (signed 'autres directions') for about 350m, then turn right at the cemetery sign.

Walk through the car-park, bearing left downhill alongside the cemetery, and then ahead down a narrow tree-lined footpath.

B This comes out in the area known as 'Petit Carhaix'. Continue ahead and then turn left across the 18th century bridge over the river Hyères into the hamlet of Kergroaz.

Here there are many attractive old cottages built of schist with rounded granite doorways.

Continue ahead and then bear left where the road divides. Shortly after, turn left.

This long quiet road runs alongside water-meadows and fields, usually full of grazing horses. The river runs parallel on the left and later comes close to the road again.

C After about 1½km, the road reaches a junction with the busy main road (D764). Cross the road carefully and turn left across the bridge, then right into a parking area. Bear right here on the path, alongside the river Hyères.

By the water here is a pretty picnic area, a good place for heron watching. Along this track there are information boards about fish in the river and fauna in the area.

Continue ahead along this path through a wooded valley for about 800m until a junction of paths near the camping site. Turn left here and then right at a fork, alongside a lake. Turn left at the junction with a small road. Walk up through the hamlet of Kerniguez and then right along a grassy triangle beside its lovely manor house (c.1744).

D The footpath swings round the back of the house and then to the left along a tarmac road to the equestrian centre. There, turn right alongside the building and follow a very narrow footpath between high banks, plunging into the trees just across the stable yard ahead.

Follow this path, which is sometimes very muddy, for about 750m and then turn left where it ends. This beautiful tree-lined hard track leads straight back to the town.

At the end of the track go straight ahead along the road and straight over at the crossroads. At the end of this residential road, turn left along a narrow road which comes out opposite the ancient church of St-Pierre de Plouguer (11th century origins), which is well worth a look. Turn right and follow the road round to the other church and the car-park.

Centre	22 CHÂTEAULIN TOWN WALK	Short

Length 3kms	Time 1½hrs	Level 2

Location & parking: CHÂTEAULIN. Park anywhere in the town centre by the river.

Refreshments: plenty of choice in the town.

The broad Aulne flows through the centre of this old town, which has long had a close connection with salmon fishing – the fish even figures on the town's coat of arms. It was an important second stage in the Nantes/Brest canal, which began at nearby Port Launay. Cafés and restaurants fill the streets and pretty flowered squares, whilst the surrounding hills provide bird's eye viewpoints over the town.

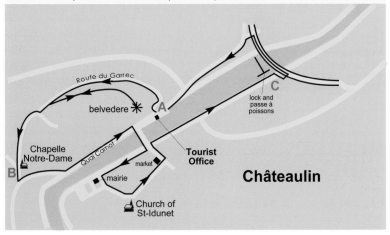

DIRECTIONS

A **Start at the tourist office, a chalet-like building with sharply sloping roofs on the quay on the north bank of the river.**

From there, cross the road to the Moulin du Roy, an old 5-storey flour-mill still in operation. Turn left and then after a few metres turn sharply right back up a narrow alley (wooden fingerpost to Belvedere). As this path, the route du Garrec, climbs, the machines working inside the mill can be seen.

Continue up this leafy lane, with the mill-stream in the valley to the right. At the signpost, turn sharply back left to the Belvedere, a viewing-platform about 250m straight ahead. (Ignore the path under the rock arch). This short detour  **is well worth it for the view of the bustling town, curving viaduct, calm river and the hills beyond. Return to the route de Garrec afterwards and bear left on uphill.**

The track is leading round the original defensive mound of the town where a castle and fortifications were built in the 10th century. The Dukes of Cornouaille chose a good spot to command the Aulne valley, although only a few stones of this edifice remain today. The castle was burnt by the English in 1373, and became a hospice from 1689 onwards.

When the track meets a road, go right, past a trio of beautiful ancient houses, one of schist with a thatched roof, relics of the 'vieux bourg' (old town), to the delightful Chapel of Notre-Dame.

The triumphal arch of the entrance dates from the second half of the 15th century. From a similar period, the calvary in front of the church has the unusual subject of the Last Judgement on its east face. The best external view of the church is from the raised viewing area opposite.

B From the steps of the church, turn left and follow the road downhill. At the next junction, turn sharply left back down to the riverside and the town.

There are good views of the castle mound above from here.

Go left along the Quai Carnot and then right over the bridge. On the other side, turn right. Continue ahead to the early 19th century marie with its unusual slated bell-tower.

From the 17th century, the town centre shifted to this bank of the river.

Take the narrow road to the left of the marie to the church.

The church of St-Idunet is a neo-gothic building of 1868. This replaced a much earlier church connected to the priory here, which was a satellite of the abbey of Landévennec. To the right of the church, set into the wall on the corner, is a stone carving of a lion (dated 1589) from the ancient priory.

Bear left in front of the church past the war memorial on the right.

There is a plaque on the wall here to Jean Moulin, sub-prefect of Châteaulin from 1930-1933, and later a resistance leader, murdered by SS man Klaus Barbie.

The market hall (halles) is in a pretty little flowered square ahead. Turn left through here back to the river and then right before the bridge along the bank to the lock just before the viaduct.

Here there is a passe à poissons (chamber for viewing fish) in the river, which is worth a look if it's open. For many centuries, Châteaulin has been a famous spot for salmon – the abbey of Landévennec held the rights to the salmon fisheries here in the 11th century.

C Cross the road and go up a little lane to the right of the viaduct to come out on the top. Turn left over the river: at the far end is a large flat terrace on the roof of the library, accessible from the road. Take the steps on the left down from the viaduct and bear left down the road back to the tourist office.

Length 5½kms	Time 2hrs	Level 2

Location & parking: SAINT-THOIS, off the D72 from Châteauneuf-du-Faou. Turn right immediately after the bridge over the Nantes/Brest canal. The car-park is about 120m on the right, by the water.

Refreshments: bar/restaurant in Saint-Thois.

This walk incorporates a particularly lovely stretch of the Aulne, in the form of the Nantes/Brest canal. The countryside around the little bourg of Saint-Thois is also very attractive and there are many fine views from the rural paths. The route includes gradual climbs but is far more relaxing than demanding.

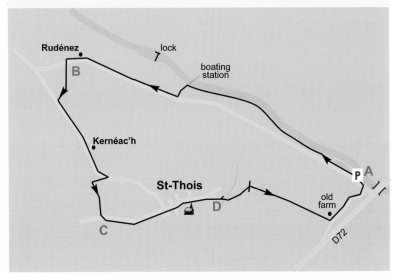

DIRECTIONS

A From the car-park, bear left along the water away from the bridge. Stay on the canal-bank for just over a kilometre before turning inland by the small boating station at Stervinou. After 100m, turn right along the

road parallel to the Aulne, with good views of the lock.

B At the next hamlet, Rudénez, bear left uphill for about 80m and then left up a narrow tree-lined path between banks. At the road, go left and continue ahead past the next hamlet in a dip. Just after the bourg sign for Saint-Thois, turn sharp right up another narrow path between hedges. Stay on this as it turns sharp left and continue ahead.

C At the road, turn left and walk downhill to the bourg. Continue straight through at the square and then bear left in front of the church. About 250m later, bear right down a steep narrow road.

D After the last house, turn right along a track over the stream. Continue ahead uphill to a major junction of paths. Here bear right on the middle one and then straight ahead.

This path, with excellent views to both sides, ends by an old farm. Turn left and continue along the front of the house and down the little road to a T-junction.

Turn left here and the car-park is just ahead on the right.

Length 6kms	**Time** 1½hrs	**Level** 1

Location & parking: near CAST (on the D7 from Châteaulin). From Cast, take the Ploéven road for about 4½kms, and stop at a small crossroads with a stone cross on the left by the hamlet of Kerhant. Park by the cross and the recycling bins.

Refreshments: none on route.

This route is a pleasant stroll through rural scenery, with good long views for much of the time. Sights of particular interest are an old chapel with its weathered calvaire and an unusual standing stone. Following country tracks, a streamside path and quiet roads, it is a straightforward and relaxing walk.

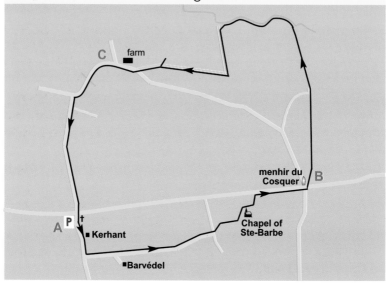

DIRECTIONS

A **Facing the stone cross by the parking, go right towards Kerhant. After about 300m, turn left to Barvédel. Where the road divides, keep straight ahead on a narrow tarmac track.**

Cross a little road and bear left on a track across an open field (just to the right of an electricity pylon). Follow this all the way to the chapel of Ste-Barbe.

The 16th century chapel of Saint Barbe has a fine calvaire dating from 1585. The Saint, (patron of firemen and miners) according to legend, was brutally tortured and killed by her own father for her faith. (A bolt of lightning then reduced him to ashes.)

Continue past the chapel to the road and turn right along it for about 400m. At the crossroads on the top of the rise, the menhir is on the left.

The celtic menhir du Cosquer, dating from c500 BC, is unusual for the horizontal slits – of unknown origin and purpose - in its stone face. Speculation includes the idea that it was a gallows at some point in its history. There is a tradition of trying to throw a small stone onto the top. If it stays there, the sky won't fall and there'll be no earthquake...

B **Go past the menhir a few paces and then bear left along a tree-lined track, which is an old Roman road. Continue ahead for 600m and then bear right at the road. This soon becomes a track and goes downhill to the stream.**

Turn left here and follow its course, keeping near the water.

After about 600m, before a row of fir trees, bear left from the stream to a track going left uphill on the edge of an open field. At the top, turn right.

Continue ahead on this path, bearing left when another track joins it, and at the road go right.

C **Past the farm, the road bends to the left and crosses a stream (wooden barriers on each side of the road). About 150m further on, bear left along a narrow road, signed Ty Bleis/Le Gorzit. Follow this all the way back to the stone cross at the starting point.**

ADDITIONAL SUGGESTIONS
for walking in Central Finistère

Here are some more good places to follow marked circuits or just to park and walk.

POULLAOUEN – where the D769 between Huelgoat and Poullaouen crosses the Aulne past Locmaria-Berrien Gare, park and walk along well-made (some ex-railway track) paths beside the river. This is a pleasant linear walk, but there is also a circular return route (Circuit de Botvarec) to Locmaria-Berrien.

ROC'H TREDUDON – there are rough car-parks on each side of the D36 on the shoulder of this Monts d'Arrée peak, and fine walks along the ridge in either direction with exceptional views.

RÉSERVOIR de ST-MICHEL – an 18km circuit (de Yeun Ellez) encircles this reservoir. (For 2kms it overlaps with Walk 14, p49.) Start from the Barrage de Nestavel, near Brennilis.

COMMANA – park by the alley grave at Mougau Bihan. The 2km Korrigan trail crosses the marshland (tourbières) on wooden walkways below the stark ridges of the Monts d'Arrée.

LAC du DRENNEC – here there is an almost level 7km circuit, mostly on well-made paths, around the lake, with fine views of the Monts d'Arrée. Swimming beaches and a crêperie are added attractions.

MÉNEZ MEUR – there are shorter trails around the animal park and nature reserve in addition to Walk 17 on page 58. (Entrance fee)

FORÊT du CRANOU – the serpentine D42 from St-Rivoal to Le Faou runs through the heart of this lovely forest, where there are many walking trails.

HANVEC – the Circuit du Plateau (5kms) explores the countryside around the ancient settlement of Hanvec (with its exceptional mairie building).

TRÉVAREZ – this well-managed park surrounding the famous 'château rose' is a good place for a leisurely walk. Take the Allée des Andromèdes from the château to the less well-known parts, and return along the Allée des Quatre  Saisons via the chapel and lake. There is always something in bloom whatever the season, and the trees are magnificent. (Entrance fee)

ROCHE du FEU – turn up by the church in Gouézec and continue to a car-park and information board at the foot of this fine view-point - a good goal for a short, steep walk.

POINTE du BINDY – beyond Logonna Daoulas, this has good views over the Bay of Daoulas and the beginning of the Aulne estuary.

LANDÉVENNEC – there is a memorable walk here (about 10kms) through the trees along the estuary to Le Loc'h and then back at a higher level through the wood and the hamlet of La Forêt.

ROSNOËN – go through here on the D47 in the direction of the Pont de Térénez and turn left after about a kilometre to the belvedere, an exceptional view-point over the Aulne estuary (see p.82). From the  parking here, the path descends through trees to the water-level, and there are marked circuits of different lengths. (NB: High water may affect part of these routes).

CHAPELLE ST-JULIEN – off the D8 shortly before entering Camaret, is the starting point for a marked 6km circuit.

CAP de la CHÈVRE – from the car-park there is a marked 9km circuit covering both sides of the wild coast here, via the hamlet of Rostudel.

THE AULNE

From its source in the Monts d'Arrée to the mouth of the estuary at Landévennec, the Aulne stretches for 144kms across Finistère. It has always provided a more fertile environment and thus greater prosperity for its region than the bleaker hills to the north.

In the early 19th century, much of the middle section with its long looping bends was incorporated by means of many locks into the Nantes/Brest canal. Originally intended for the movement of troops and supplies, it became better used for the transport of agricultural and industrial products. Quarries still line sections of the canal today (see Walk 19). In 1826 the first loads of slate were moved from Châteaulin to Port Launay at the western end of the canal.

Beyond that, the Pont de Térénez bridges the river for access to the Presqu'île de Crozon (Crozon peninsula). It opened in 1952, an earlier bridge on this site having been blown up by the Germans in 1944.

A little way downstream is a ships' graveyard, which can be seen from the viewpoint (Belvédère de Gorrequer) near Landévennec. Originally chosen in 1840 for its calm, deep waters as a temporary resting place for large vessels, it later became the final port of call for many ships.

The mouth of the estuary is at Landévennec, where there are the remains of a famous ancient abbey, twice destroyed by Vikings, on the waterfront.

The Aulne has always been known as a salmon river (see Walk 22) and today it still provides excellent fishing as well as rich and varied scenery for walkers.

South	25 FORÊT DE CARNOËT	Long

Length 13kms	Time 4½hrs	Level 3

Location & parking: from QUIMPERLÉ, take the D783 toward Pont Aven but turn off left almost immediately on the D49 to Le Pouldu. After 1½ kms take a small turning on the left (signed La Métairie) and continue past the chapel at Lothéa to a car-park about 350m further on.

Refreshments: none on route, but there is a crêperie, in season, near the Abbey of St-Maurice (detour).

This forest is a remarkably beautiful place to walk at any time of year. Certain parts are well-used for riding, jogging and cycling, but the long stretch down the Laïta estuary is usually a haven of tranquillity.

The going is easy, on well-made paths, and there is much of interest to discover. If the 5km detour does not appeal, don't fail to visit the Abbey of St Maurice at the southern end of the forest by car and enjoy its exceptional setting.

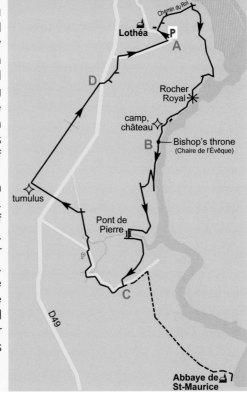

DIRECTIONS

A **From the car-park, walk back up the road for 150m and turn right just before the first house. Go straight ahead where the path divides soon after. Bear right at the next fork for a long gradual descent.**

This is the Chemin du Roi, a 13th century route established by Jean Le Roux, Duke of Brittany. This forest was a ducal, and later regal, hunting and fishing domain, although commoners also had right of access to the woods. Originally the path had high walls on each side, a measure to keep animals within the forest bounds.

At the bottom, turn right uphill for about 60m and then left through the forest. Bear left at a junction of paths on a stony track. The path then bears right for a long stretch down the banks of the river. Continue straight ahead.

The Laïta estuary is to the left here, but the main river channel

is on the far side, and water levels are also affected by the state of the tides. Islets and vegetation have grown up in what was originally a very broad estuary. Small quays such as the Port de la Véchène were once used to ship logs to Lorient from the forest. Only a few large stones remain today. Across the Laïta is the Bothané Château.

Take the left fork signed to the Rocher Royal, a rocky viewpoint above the estuary. The path then returns downhill. Follow it behind a house on the waterside further on and then continue ahead through a wooden barrier.

To the right here are the remains of an ancient fortified camp and then the stones of a former château.

B **Shortly after, to the right of the path, is the rock formation known as the Bishop's Throne. About 400m beyond that, at a clearing with a crossroads of paths, turn sharp right back uphill. This narrow path among the pines soon swings back to** the left. At a T-junction turn left on a wider, earth track. Follow this same track all the way down to the Pont de Pierre. Over the bridge, bear left uphill. At a narrow tarmac road, turn right.

DETOUR (2x2½kms): turn left here and follow the track all the way to the ruins of the Abbey of St-Maurice in its idyllic lakeside setting. Then retrace the route to this junction and continue the walk.

C **Continue ahead on the road for about 1km, down into a stream valley and up again. At the top near a parking area where the road bends left, take the track to the right, past a wooden barrier. Almost immediately, leave this track to follow a narrow path straight ahead downhill. Cross the stream and, at the track on the other side, turn left. Continue ahead for about 400m. At a crossroads of paths, turn left (signed Moëlan). Cross the main road (D49) and go straight ahead. After about 350m, turn right by the tumulus.**

The tumulus of Kerquilven is a simple mound to the left of the path at the junction, long ago dug right out to the extent that now you can walk right through it!

Follow this long track straight ahead for about 1½kms back to the D49. (This involves crossing a steep-sided stream valley: a detour via the GR is possible.)

D **Cross the road and take the path ahead, which** almost immediately bears left by a wooden barrier. Just after, where the path divides, go left. At the next fork, bear left again and keep straight ahead. In a clearing bear slightly left and towards buildings visible through the trees.

When the path comes out onto a small road by a wooden barrier, turn right. The starting point car-park is about 650m ahead, past the equestrian centre.

Length 12kms	**Time** 3½hrs	**Level** 1

Location & parking: near COMBRIT (between Pont l'Abbé and Bénodet). Turn off the D44, 1½kms west of the Pont de Cornouaille, (right from Pont l'Abbé direction, left from the bridge) signed to the hamlet of Kermor, and then immediately right into the car-park.

Refreshments: crêperie, café and restaurant in Ste-Marine.

This varied walk crosses the polder (land below sea-level reclaimed by drainage techniques) which is now a protected natural site with interesting flora and fauna. The route also includes a long stretch of glorious beach and the charming small port of Ste-Marine, before returning to the start by wooded lanes. It is a pretty level walk and should present little problem even in poor weather.

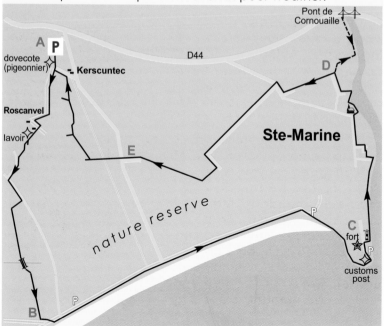

DIRECTIONS

Before setting out it is worth taking the steps in the centre of the car-park up to an observation post with views to the sea.

A Leave the car-park from the far end and visit the pigeonnier of Kerscuntec just ahead.

This restored pigeonnier once belonged to the castle of Cosquer, a 16th century building just north of here, demolished in 1975. According to a local legend, a horse brought back from China in the 19th century was buried in the pigeonnier and its ghost appears each night of the full moon. In 1989 workmen actually discovered the remains of small horse here.

Bear left from the pigeonnier to join a narrow tarmac lane on a bend, and go right. Follow this lane all the way to the hamlet of Roscanvel. Go behind the houses and, at a crossroads of paths, turn right.

To the right of this tree-lined path soon after is a large stone lavoir where women used to wash clothes in the open air.

Follow the narrow path along a raised bank above the marshes. At the end, go through a wooden barrier and bear left, then continue ahead straight across an open field to a small road.

Turn left here and continue ahead for about 150m round a bend to the next junction. Turn left again onto a straight road

(which goes all the way down to the beach, if a short-cut is needed). After about 300m, turn right on a path alongside the tennis courts. Then turn left and continue ahead over the polder, crossing a small bridge and ignoring other paths.

B When the path finishes, bear left for a few steps and then turn left again on a wide, flat track. The coastal path here is separated from the sea by high dunes (because of the nature of the polder), so for the next 2kms, either follow this or walk along the fine beach running parallel.

At the end of the beach (or from the track, bear right through the car-park) continue on the sandy coastal path out to the Pointe de Combrit and an old stone customs house.

C From there follow the road out of the car-park for about 100m. Turn right along a footpath.

Before turning, notice on the left an old fort of Napoleon III (from 1862), now transformed into an arts centre.

The path runs down the side of the lighthouse and then along the Odet estuary. Remain on this path, which eventually runs along the edge of a public park and then turns left, inland.

The lighthouse seen from the car park.

After about 200m, turn right past a metal barrier and right again at the next one, and then left soon after at a T-junction. Then turn right at the next T-junction.

Continue ahead for about 400m to the Chapelle de Ste-Marine. Go down the steps beside the chapel and continue left along by the harbour, past a crêperie and restaurant. The path then bears right along the harbour wall to the Café de la Cale.

Go up the narrow stone steps to the left immediately beyond the café building and then ahead to the road. Turn right and continue for about 200m to where the path forks.

DETOUR (2x1km): continue on the right fork up to the Pont de Cornouaille and back for a beautiful waterside route.

D To continue the walk, go left at the fork and follow a tree-lined path between houses. Where it opens out, continue ahead on the same path. At the road continue straight ahead for about 150m to a T-junction and turn right. Turn left into the route de Béréven soon after.

Follow this road to the end and then round to the left. Just before a house a few metres ahead, turn right down a straight track.

At the bottom of the slope, turn right before the plank bridge. Follow the track, which eventually becomes a road and bears left.

E At the next junction go straight over (signed allée cavalière), a most attractive woodland route. Past the wooden barrier, continue ahead.

Ignore a long straight crosspath (the allée cavalière) and at a fork in the path soon after, bear right through a wooden barrier and follow a path lined by tall pine trees.

At a junction of paths, go straight on and at the next, bear right before the wooden post. Follow the path round and then straight ahead. A white slash on the tree to the right of the path denotes the 'sentier éducatif', which has numbered information posts.

At the next junction bear right and then straight ahead through trees. Continue ahead right up to the hamlet of Kerscuntec. At the road turn left back to the pigeonnier about 200m ahead.

Length 14kms	Time 4hrs	Level 1

Location & parking: from Quimper, take the D156 to Plounéour-Lanvern. Then go towards St-Jean-Trolimon (D57) and follow one of several signs off this road to the right for the Chapelle de Tronoan. Park opposite the chapel.

Refreshments: possibly in season, but own provisions advised.

This is an unexacting walk with open views, streams, a pretty chapel in a wooded valley, and constant awareness of the vast Bay of Audierne. It is a good route for bird-watching, including an observation post over two coastal lakes and the surrounding reedy marsh. The last main stretch is along the incredibly impressive beach, where Atlantic breakers thunder in, often to the accompaniment of a roaring wind.

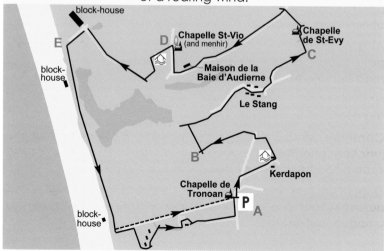

The Chapel of Tronoan has one of the oldest calvaries (c.1450) in Brittany, impressive even though weather-worn. The numerous figures are finely portrayed, especially Mary, who looks, with her long, loose hair and exposed breasts, more earthy goddess than Holy Virgin of the Church. The chapel is often called the 'cathedral of the dunes'.

DIRECTIONS

A Walk back up the road from the car-park for a few metres and take the road on the left, signed R2, towards Plounéour-Lanvern. After 150m, turn right onto a track to Kerdapon.

After the little stone fountain on the left of the path, turn left and follow a long grassy track, with excellent views across to the sea. At the narrow road, turn right and then left almost immediately where the footpath is signed. This heads straight towards the coast.

B When the grassy track ends, there is a cross-path. (But no marker, at the time of research. Directly left is the Chapelle de Tronoan.) Turn right here – there is a wooden marker about 150m ahead.

At a narrow gravel cross-path, turn right and follow a pretty path beside a little stream. This becomes a narrow tarmac road into the hamlet of Le Stang.

Note the stone cottages here, thatched with local reeds of the marais.

Continue ahead through the hamlet, bearing left at the junction, and then take the next turning on the left. This road soon becomes a grassy track with open views.

C Just past an orange marker, turn left on a rough path across a field. The chapel of St Evy is directly ahead, over a wooden foot-bridge.

The chapel was built in 1660, in honour of St Evy who came from Britain in the 7th century. The Pardon (annual religious festival with procession) is held on the first Sunday after assumption (Aug 15).

Continue ahead up a gentle slope from the chapel and bear left opposite the noticeboard.

At the next junction, turn first left along a straight track. Continue ahead for 1½kms.

On the right is a group of buildings, including the Maison de la Baie d'Audierne in an attractive low stone house. Exhibitions are held here in the summer.

To the left is the Étang de St-Vio. This lake is a good spot for bird-watching, with observation posts.

Follow the road round to the right and the Chapelle St-Vio is visible ahead.

This is an unusual little building with a large stone basin outside, and note the stone steps on each side of the roof to reach the bell-tower. Just past the chapel is a small rounded menhir.

D **Turn left onto a footpath just past the menhir. After about 150m, a tiny fountain is on the left of the path.**

Continue ahead, following a wiggle in the path over a plank bridge and along an overgrown grassy track. The route is tortuous here, but the goal is the huge block-house clearly visible away to the right. Although the path seems to be going quite the wrong way at times, continue and at a major junction of paths turn right.

Just before the fortifications ahead and the small lake on the right, turn left on a path leading directly to the magnificent beach (plage) of the bay of Audierne.

From the beach, Audierne itself is to the right, together with the long line of Cap-Sizun ending in the Pointe du Raz. To the left is the Pointe de la Torche, where there is a fine Neolithic alley-grave, and the headland of Penmarc'h with its lighthouse behind.

E Turn left and walk either on the dunes for views of the sea on one side and the Loc'h ar Stang on the other, or simply stick to the beach. Pass one block-house almost straight away, make for the next, about 2kms ahead, and then go through the dunes and the car-park.

Then there is a choice-

EITHER: take the road leading straight back up to the starting point at the Chapelle de Tronoan, visible ahead.

OR: after 100m up the road, turn right onto a track. This goes ahead for about 250m and then bends left round the last house.

Continue ahead for a short distance and then turn left onto a footpath. Look out for a faint track along a bank on the right. At the end bear left round the front of a small gite complex and turn right along a track. This turns to the right soon after. At the next junction, go left. At the top of this green track, turn left along the road to the chapel.

South	28 GOYEN ESTUARY	Long

Length 12kms	Time 4hrs	Level 2

Location & parking: AUDIERNE, from the bridge over the Goyen estuary. Park anywhere central, near the harbour and bridge.

Refreshments: plenty of choice in Audierne (start and finish) and Pont Croix (half-way).

This route takes in the glorious Goyen estuary, linking two very different, but equally interesting, towns. Start in the busy harbour of Audierne and then follow the wide river inland to Pont Croix with its fine old buildings and stepped streets. For a very relaxing day, walk out in the morning, have a leisurely lunch in Pont Croix and then enjoy an afternoon stroll back down the estuary. There is a wealth of bird life to observe along the way.

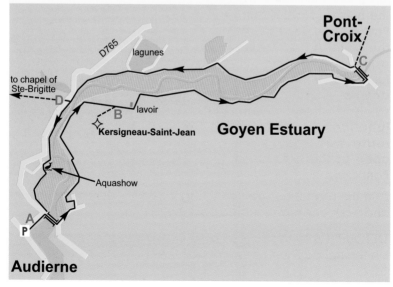

DIRECTIONS

A From the harbour in Audierne, cross the bridge and take the road immediately to the left. After about 400m, turn left again along the access road to the hotel. After 100m, take the narrow footpath (signed

sentier côtier) sharp left downhill through the trees.

NOTE: This coastal path follows the line of the river at various levels all the way to Pont Croix. From time to time, the path bears slightly right and runs parallel with the river behind hedges. It is important to observe these sections to conserve the fragile river banks.

After about 2kms, the path climbs quite steeply for a short way inland. Near the top of the rise, there is a small clearing.

> DETOUR (2x125m): take the path to the right here to see the archaeological site of Kersigneau-Saint-Jean. Here there are the remains of an iron age enclosure and later gallo–romano settlement.

B From the clearing, keep straight ahead on the narrow coastal path. Past an old stone lavoir, the path drops steeply again. Stay on it, following all the ups and downs and going straight ahead at any junction of paths. The route becomes more open as the path nears Pont Croix.

Join the road and bear left along it. At the T-junction turn left and walk across the bridge past the old mills.

> DETOUR: take the stepped passageway (Petite rue chère) on the right a short distance over the bridge uphill to see the town.

Pont Croix was once the main centre of the whole Cap-Sizun peninsula and it has many fine buildings from that earlier period. There is a local heritage museum in an exceptionally fine house from the 15th century (Le Marquisat), and the church of Notre-Dame de Roscudon is also worth seeing.

C Once over the bridge, bear left immediately along a narrow tarmac road which soon turns into a wide track, running near the river, through a public park.

Continue ahead on this track. After about 2kms, join the road and bear left, past the parking and then ahead on the track again. Carry on alongside the river at the next road not long after, past the 'lagunes'.

The last stretch to Audierne is on an old railway line.

D About a kilometre later, over a little bridge, the path comes out into a parking area by the D765.

DETOUR (about 3kms): cross the road here for a circular walk in the Bois de Suguensou to the little chapel of Ste-Brigitte.

To continue the walk, go straight ahead along the track by the river.

The path is now called the Promenade de Penryn, after the town in Cornwall which is twinned with Audierne.

The path moves away from the river via an old railway cutting.

At the road, bear left and then left just past the Aquarium (L'Aquashow) to join a path by the river again. This narrows past the slipway of the little harbour to come out on the bridge at the starting point.

| **Length** 9½kms | **Time** 3hrs | **Level** 2 |

Location & parking: PORTEC, south of Moëlan-sur-Mer. From Moëlan take the D24 (direction Clohars-Carnoët). About 1km south, at a mini-roundabout, go straight ahead to Portec. Stay on this minor road for 3kms, through St-Thamec and then, just after the hamlet sign for Kerampellan, turn right on a small road, signed Portec. Continue ahead for about 800m, past the no through road sign, to a car-park at the end of the track.

Refreshments: none on route.

This circuit is quite off the beaten track and should provide a peaceful walk. The coastal path weaves in and out of sheltered creeks and then up the wooded Merrien estuary, where there is a small harbour with colourful boats and oyster beds. The return route inland crosses a gentle stream valley and passes through houses and past an old stone lavoir before winding seawards again down a grassy lane.

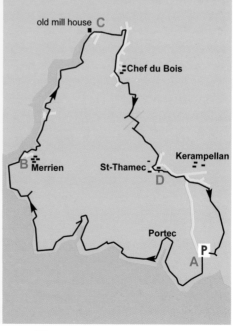

DIRECTIONS

A From the car-park, take the track on the right between two low posts. At the coast, turn right. After a level walk along the cliffs, the path turns inland to follow the line of a creek. Walk round this and bear left on the coastal path.

The path forks, but soon rejoins. Continue ahead to the next inlet and go round the creek, then bear left to continue along the coast. Where the path divides, bear left.

B At a stone wall, the path turns right up the river Merrien estuary. At a junction of paths, bear left. Go left again where the path divides. At a crossroads of paths, go straight ahead.

The path comes out in the little harbour of Merrien. Walk through to the other end where the path goes along the harbour wall. Continue ahead on a tree-lined path.

At a little road, go ahead and then turn left after 120m, back onto the coastal path. When the path bends inland, turn left soon after by a wooden post.

C At the head of the estuary, go straight ahead past the old mill house and ahead on a path through barriers where the road goes right.

When the path meets a road, turn right and then right again at a crossroads. Continue for about 500m into the hamlet of Chef du Bois. Where the road forks, bear left and then left again along a track. Keep on this path until a fork, then turn left downhill between high banks.

Cross the stream and continue ahead. After the path swings right, go left at a T-junction of paths. Turn right at a junction by thatched cottages, and right at the next junction. After about 50m, turn left and then, immediately on left, just past the house on the corner, take a narrow grassy footpath.

D At a junction of paths, bear left downhill, past a stone lavoir. Turn right at the road and right just past the Kerampellan hamlet sign. Turn left and then bear right where the road forks. It soon turns into a grassy footpath between hedges. Stay on this path, keeping the fields to the right until a T-junction of paths. Turn right back to the car-park.

Length 10kms	**Time** 3hrs	**Level** 1

Location & parking: RAGUÉNEZ. From Névez, follow signs to Raguénez Plage (beach) and park near the island.

Refreshments: good café on route in season, and hotel by the parking at the start.

This undemanding circuit begins right on the coast, with an option to swim before or after from fine sandy beaches by the car-park. It can also be extended by up to 2km, if the tide is low, by walking out across the rocks and then right round Raguénez island, just off-shore.

The walk starts along the coastal path and then cuts inland to the charming hamlet of Kerascoët, with its famous thatched cottages. A quiet cross-country route finally returns to Raguénez through further hamlets before a last stretch along the shore.

DIRECTIONS

A **Facing the sea, go left along the front to the entrance to the quay. Take the coastal path to the left and follow this all the way along above the beach (or on the**

Looking back to Raguénez island

sand if preferred). At another car-park, bear right on the coastal path, which drops down to wooden barriers and then rises to round the headland.

B **At a fork in the path, turn left inland alongside a large hedge and conifers. Go straight ahead at the road, and where it swings right, continue ahead on a grassy track. At a fork, go ahead between houses. At a T-junction turn left and follow the gravel track. At the end, turn right, and walk ahead through the cottages.**

The hamlet of Kerascoët is famous for its picturesque chaumières (thatched cottages). A feature of their construction unique to this area is the incorporation at

ground level of large upright slabs of granite (men zao in Breton). There is also an excellent, friendly café, the Île Verte, which has outdoor seating in season. Opposite is a large communal bread-oven.

C **At the T-junction beyond the hamlet, turn left and almost immediately right down the side of a camping site. At a junction of paths, turn left by the wooden fingerpost. (In a grassy clearing just ahead there is a simple fontaine to the right). Follow the track and continue ahead where it joins a road.**

Turn sharp right at the next junction (signed Rouz Trémorvézen), and where the road divides, go left.

DETOUR (2x150m): to see the plain stone Fontaine de Rouz Trémorvézen, go straight ahead and then return.

Continue ahead where the houses end and the track turns into a grassy lane. Stay on this route for about one kilometre, to an open space with large rocks, at the top of a very slight rise.

D Turn left here, along a similar track. At the road, cross and go straight ahead along another track. Pass a stagnant lake on the left and then just stay on the track until it becomes a road. At the camping site, continue ahead to the road junction. Turn left  here and then, almost immediately, right down a track, past a vehicle no-entry sign.

Where the track bends right, leave it and go straight ahead to another track. Stay on this to the road and then turn right.

E Walk ahead up to a junction by a stone calvary and then turn left. After about 30m, turn right by the wooden fingerpost.

Follow this road for about 300m and then turn right along a wide grassy path. This track runs between fields and comes out at a picnic area beside the road.

Turn left here, and after about 300m, left again down a narrow road with a fingerpost and stone wall on the right.

Continue ahead where this tarmac road turns into a track and then bear left by the fire hydrant. Just before some gates, the path turns right. At the road, turn left and follow it round to the right to a T-junction with another road. Turn right here and walk down towards the sea ahead.

F Turn left before the car-park and cross the road to get onto the coastal path along the top of the rocks above the beach. Follow this all the way back to the next car-park and the starting-point.

Raguénez island as seen at the end of the walk.

Length 9kms	**Time** 3hrs	**Level** 2

Location & parking: POULDREUZIC, west of Quimper, on the D40 via Pluguffan. Park in the car-park near the church.

Refreshments: in Pouldreuzic, but none on route.

This rural route starts rather unremarkably, but in fact includes some very beautiful paths and several large standing stones in exceptional settings. The detour is highly recommended for this reason. The walk also passes a gallic stele and a very attractive old river ford. In or after bad weather some tracks here will be very muddy indeed.

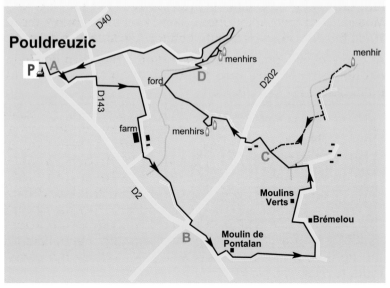

DIRECTIONS

A From the car-park, turn right down the street past the church and then left along the rue de la Mairie. Take the second turning on the right, rue de Poul Bolic, and then turn left at the end of the road.

Continue ahead to the main road (D143). Turn right and then almost immediately left along a green track beside a very high evergreen hedge.

At the end, turn right and follow the narrow road. Where it forks, bear right and then keep on this road through a large farm complex. At a T-junction, bear right and then immediately left down a narrow path between high banks.

After about 100m, the path deviates briefly up onto the left bank to bridge a stream. Continue ahead through two wooden posts. On joining a track, go straight on and follow this all the way to a road. Turn right to the junction with the D2.

B Turn left along the main road for about 400m and then turn left (signed Moulin de Pontalan). Follow this road past the houses and go ahead when it becomes a track.

Continue straight ahead for about 800m to a narrow road and turn left along it. Continue past houses at Brémelou and Moulins Verts, until, after about 500m, where the road turns at 90° to the right towards a large hamlet, turn left down a track.

At a fork go straight on down to a stream and then continue ahead on the narrow path for about 250m to a junction of paths before the next hamlet.

DETOUR (2 x 1km): go right here and stay on the same path, which eventually swings right over a little stream. Go up the hill ahead to a track and turn left. Follow this for about another 500m to the edge of a field. The menhirs are to the right here in a secluded hollow. Return by the same route to rejoin the walk.

C Follow the path ahead past the buildings. Bear left and then right at a little road. At the T-junction turn right and then left soon after along a track.

After about 400m, there is an opening into the field with the Gallic stele. Follow the path round the top of the field and then right just past the stele into a group of trees.

Here, according to legend, Saint Kodelig lived and then left his 'butter'(the stele), 'wardrobe'(the menhir) and 'bed'(the lying stone).

Follow the path ahead (menhir on the left) and then right in a loop back to the main path. Turn left before the information board.

Continue ahead on this path for about a kilometre, swinging sharp right by a picturesque little ford.

D At the road go left for about 60m and then turn right along a track just before the seat. At a fork in the path, bear right. After about 250m, the menhirs are to the right by a stream.

Return to the path, which soon turns back on itself along the edge of a field. Follow this straight ahead back towards the town.

At the little road go left, follow the road round to the right soon after, then bear left and ahead through a series of hamlets to the D143. Cross straight over here into the rue de la Mairie and follow it all the way back to the church and the car-park.

South	32 POINTE DU VAN	Medium

Length 10kms	**Time** 3½hrs	**Level** 4

Location & parking: D7 from Douarnenez (turn left before the Pointe du Van to the Baie des Trépassés) or D784 from Quimper (turn right before Pointe du Raz to Baie des Trépassés). Park at the Baie des Trépassés.

Refreshments: two hotels at the starting point (not open all year); none on route.

This walk starts and ends at the magnificent Baie des Trépassés (Bay of the Dead) between the Pointe du Raz and the Pointe du Van, two fine rocky promontories. The route begins inland with views of Lake Laoual and then joins the coast path on the northern side with its craggy cliffs and sea views. The path has plenty of ups and downs and requires care, especially on the last section past the chapel of St-They.

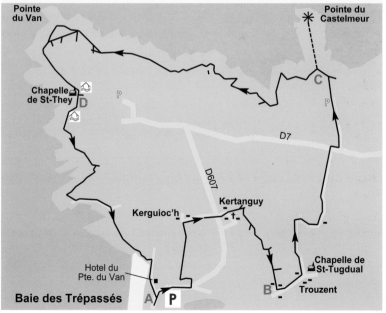

DIRECTIONS

A Facing away from the sea, go left along the road (D607), with the Hotel de la Pointe du Van to the left. On the next bend, turn left beside a house and then stay on this grassy path.

At the hamlet of Kerguioc'h, follow the road round to the right and ahead, crossing the D607, to the hamlet of Kertanguy. Here take a track to the left past the stone cross.

Follow this downhill. Bear right at a fork, and right again a few paces after. At the next fork, bear left, slightly uphill. At a junction of paths, bear right slightly downhill again. Then stay on the main green path, ignoring minor paths off, until another fork by a stone wall and fir trees. Here bear right downhill.

B When the track comes out in a hamlet, bear left and then left again at a road junction shortly after. Go ahead through the hamlet of Trouzent to the Chapel of St-Tugdual, with its pretty fontaine and lavoir.

Just before the chapel, take the road uphill, which becomes a track. After a 90° bend, bear right at a fork. Go straight on to the road. Turn left and follow it up to the D7. Turn right here and then left just after (to Pointe du Castelmeur). This road becomes a track and goes through a parking area ahead towards the point.

C Bear left along the coastal path, to continue the walk.

DETOUR (2x350m): turn right along a narrow path to go out to the end of the craggy Pointe du Castelmeur, once an Iron Age fort. Return to the coastal path.

Follow the narrow coastal path through the heather and across the rocks all the way to the Pointe du Van. The way is usually obvious on the ground, but it does not matter if you choose an alternative path, as long as you continue to progress along the cliffs towards the point about 2kms ahead.

Note the following: At a fork of paths by a stone wall, don't miss the right fork, marked with a red and white slash on a post.

Near to the Pointe du Van itself, the gravel path is properly made and has low fencing to encourage visitors to keep away from the edge of the cliffs for conservation as well as safety.

Where the path opens out and others join it, continue along the cliff-top. At a fork soon after, take either route round the point. Signs to the chapel appear soon after.

The chapel of St-They has been restored recently. Notice in the precinct an unusual plain pillar with simple male and female figures. There is a fontaine (of St-Mathieu) nearby and another, more elaborately enclosed, further on.

D After the chapel, bear right along the coastal path and past another fontaine. Here there are excellent views of the Pointe du Raz and across to the Île de Sein on a clear day.

Continue on the coast path through many steep and rocky sections, requiring careful attention around a cove packed with huge grass-covered rocks. Cross a tiny stream and bear left for a gentler ascent up the cliff.

Further round this same cove, after a steep descent, follow a wide grassy path for a few paces and then take the narrow earth path downhill on the right. Step over another little stream and then bear left for another rocky scramble.

Continue straight ahead and then bear left down to the narrow road below.

Turn left along it for about 400m, then turn right along the coastal path again. At a clear fork in the path after about 150m, either bear left up over the headland, or bear right round the coast for a longer, more precarious, walk.

At the Baie des Trépassés, the path comes down quite steeply to join the road behind the Hotel de la Pointe du Van. Turn right along it to the parking areas.

Length 4kms	Time 1½hrs	Level 2

Location & parking: PONT AVEN. Park anywhere near the centre.

Refreshments: plenty of choice in the town.

The walk starts in the centre of this pretty little town on the Aven and then goes up to the Bois d'Amour - a place of inspiration for many painters - for a wooded walk, returning along a riverside path. There is also a short linear section to include a visit to the delightful Chapelle de Trémalo, which is well worth seeing.

DIRECTIONS

A From the bridge in the centre of the town, go along rue Émile Bernard for about 50m and then right along the Promenade Xavier Grall, a picturesque walkway over the Aven.

Xavier Grall was born in Landivisiau in 1930, and returned to Finistère after a journalistic career in Paris. He made a passionate contribution to modern Breton literature in prose and poetry. His memorial plaque is in the little garden here.

Turn left at a 'crossroads' of bridges, and then right uphill. Where the road forks, go left, and bear left again soon after. At the road, go straight across into the wood. Then bear left uphill.

The Bois d'Amour was a favourite spot for painters of the 'Pont Aven School', influenced by Gauguin. He gave famous advice here to Paul Sérusier about the use of colour in painting nature. A painting of the wood by Émile Bernard is in the Musée des Beaux Arts in Quimper.

B At the top, go right and stay on the road all the way up to a T-junction. Then go left to the chapel.

The Chapelle de Trémalo is beautiful in its simplicity. Above the nave hangs the 17th century figure which inspired Gauguin's painting The Yellow Christ.

Return by the same route and then turn left along the top of the wood, by a radio mast. Stay on this path, which starts to go downhill after about 800m.

C Follow the sharp right bend back along the river, and, after a few metres on a narrow road, go right, before the metal bridge, along the riverbank.

At the end, go under the bridge and then left down the road to return to the centre of the town.

Length 5kms	Time 1½hrs	Level 2

Location & parking: near CONCARNEAU. Outside the town, follow the D783 (direction Trégunc/Quimperlé) over the bridge and turn left soon after onto the D22 (direction Melgven). Bear left where the road forks and about one kilometre later, turn left (sign to hamlet of le Brunec). There is a large white building (water purification plant) in the valley here. Park before the bridge, near the information board.

Refreshments: none on route.

This is a straightforward route along the tree-lined banks of the wide Moros river, with attractive waterside paths and good opportunities for bird-watching. It would make a peaceful contrast to a visit to the walled 'ville close' in Concarneau. Although the walk is not difficult, there are quite a few wooden or stone steps – almost all with handrails - that require care.

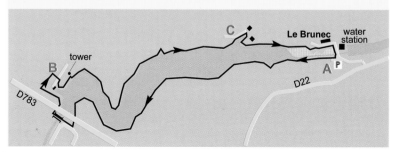

DIRECTIONS

A Facing the information board, go to the left down a narrow tarmac road alongside the stream, then straight ahead on the footpath.

Continue on this route all along the estuary. After about 1½kms, the river sweeps round to the right and then left under the high road bridge.

The footpath here bears right alongside a road beneath the bridge and then over a footbridge.

Stay on the path which soon bears left and climbs away from the water, runs parallel with the main D783 for a short distance and then begins to descend to the right.

B Turn right by the sign (Sentier Côtier) to continue downhill. At the bottom, turn right onto the track and then almost immediately take the narrow path to the left of a fence. Continue ahead and then go sharp right down steps just before a little tower. Stay on this path near the water for about a kilometre.

C Bear right where it meets a track. After about 80m, turn sharp right in front of a house back towards the river and then continue ahead.

After about 500m, the path joins a track in front of a house. Follow this ahead up to the water station, where it turns right at 90° to return to the starting point.

Length 4kms	**Time** 1½hrs	**Level** 2

Location & parking: near QUIMPER. From the D15 (direction Corlay) turn left to Lestonan and then continue ahead to Quélennec. The site of Stangala is signed to the right off the rue de Quélennec. Turn along the narrow allée du Stangala and follow this single-track road for about 700m. There is a large car-park at the end.

Refreshments: none on route.

This is a site of outstanding natural beauty and the directions include two highly recommended detours. Here the lovely Odet river, broad and fast-flowing, wends its way down to Quimper through an impressive gorge. The walk begins on the hill-top above the river and then descends through woods to the water-side. It is not a difficult walk – the path zig-zags back and forward to alleviate the gradient and there are no steep climbs.

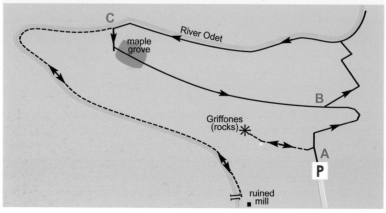

DIRECTIONS

A From the parking, follow the path ahead into the trees. After about 250m, the path forks.

DETOUR (2x450m): take the left fork and follow the path to the rocks at the end for a spectacular view over the river and the gorge. Return to the fork and turn left downhill.

The rocks are above the cave of a legendary dragon which once terrorised the area. He devoured a monthly tribute of a young girl, until an impoverished knight discovered that the beautiful maiden he had long loved from afar, was the next chosen victim. He killed the dragon, but was touched by its poisonous breath and fell seriously ill. In his absence, a rival claimed to have overcome the monster and was to marry the girl. The poor knight struggled to the church on the day of the wedding and produced the dragon's tongue, which he had cut out, to claim his bride.

The rocks are still called the Griffones, and gargoyles in the shape of dragons and griffons can be seen at the nearby 16th century Chapel of Saint-Guénolé.

Continue ahead downhill.

B After about 450m, turn right down a path by a wooden post. Continue downhill to the river and then bear left along it.

After a little over a kilometre, the river bends to the left. About 400m further on there is a junction of paths by a wooden post and a seat near the water.

DETOUR (2x1km): for a different aspect of this beautiful river, continue ahead along the bank to a bridge over the water. The river is enclosed by woods on this stretch and full of granite boulders. There are further paths in the woods opposite for longer exploration: otherwise, return to the last junction.

C Turn left here onto a track through fir trees. After about 300m, bear left onto a green path through a maple grove. This path leads all the way back up to the car-park.

South	36 DOUARNENEZ	Short

Length 4kms	Time 1½hrs	Level 2

Location & parking: DOUARNENEZ. Park in the town centre. There is a car-park in rue de Port Rhu behind the tourist office.

Refreshments: wide choice in Douarnenez or take a picnic to the Plomarc'h.

Douarnenez is a working port with many interesting buildings and atmospheric streets. This walk contrasts the bustle of the town and the activities of the Port de Rosmeur with the haven of the Plomarc'h, a beautifully peaceful green area of little coves, historic hamlets, archaeological remains and a small farm specialising in rare breeds of domestic farm animals.

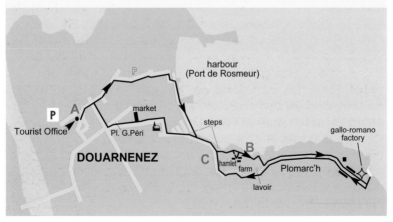

DIRECTIONS

A From the Tourist Office, go left. At the traffic lights, go straight across and take the second road on the right (rue du Quartier Maître Guillou).

Follow this to a small open square (Place des Pêcheurs) and go (almost) straight ahead down rue Boudoulec. At the bottom, turn right to come out by the harbour. Go right along the quay to some steps at the very end.

At the top turn left to the Plomarc'h, about 175m ahead. Here go left down the steps just before the entrance sign.

A short way ahead is a tiny hamlet to the right of the path. Turn off to see the old houses, some ruined, which once housed rope-makers and basket-weavers. There were twenty-three houses here in the early 19th century.

B Continue on the path, past a small orchard, and then go left at a junction of paths. At intervals there are paths and steps down to little beaches on the left. Further on are open green spaces with excellent views over the bay.

After about 500m, the path reaches another group of very old houses. Just beyond these on the left is an important site.

This exceptional gallo-romano 'factory' for making garum (pungent fish-sauce) dates from the 3rd-4th centuries AD.

Retrace the route. At the fork shortly before the first hamlet, go left past the 'Grand Lavoir' and ahead past the fowl pens and some wooden barriers to an outbuilding on the left with information about the breeds of animals.

Follow the path round, past the playground (on the right) and then bear right to return to the entrance to the Plomarc'h.

C Go ahead along the road and then at the fork bear left uphill. Take the third road on the right (rue Antoine Cariou) and then turn left up past the church and the market hall.

Continue to the Place Gabriel Péri, where there is an Egyptian-style statue on a pillar, and then go right along rue Jean Bart. Take the next turning on the left at the traffic lights to return to the starting point.

ADDITIONAL SUGGESTIONS
for walking in South Finistère

Here are some more good places to follow marked circuits or just to park and walk.

FORÊT de CARNOËT – this is a perfect spot for short walks, from any of the car-parks at the northern end, or the Abbey of St-Maurice at the south. (NB: for a long walk here, see p. 83)

QUIMPERLÉ – historical town walk of 4kms.

BÉLON estuary – follow signs to the Port of Bélon and the beautiful Bélon estuary, famous for its oysters. Here there is a 9km marked Circuit du Port de Bélon via the coastal path, and several shorter circuits.

MELLAC – Park at the very interesting and well-presented Manoir de Kernault, signed from Mellac and the D765. A marked trail of about 2½kms begins along the back of the manor house.

BANNALEC – there is a walking circuit from the Chapel of St-Cado (off the D765 east of Bannalec).

Chapel of St-Cado

SCAËR – just south-west of the town, almost on the Morbihan border, is the Forest of Coat Loc'h. Park by the Maison du Garde in the forest and follow a marked trail of just over 3kms for easy forest walking, with sites of historical interest on route. Longer trails are also available in the forest.

ROSPORDEN – park near the church and follow a trail of nearly 4kms around the town's lakes, with sights of historic interest on route.

BOIS de PLEUVEN, just off the N165, east of Quimper. This has a woodland circuit of 10kms.

QUIMPER – from the cathedral, cross the river and climb the steep paths of Mt Frugy (behind the tourist office). Then continue along the river to Locmaria, one of the oldest quarters of the city, with an ancient church and working potteries.

TREFFIAGAT – south from the village to Lehan and a car-park at the beach. Here there is a 7km Circuit of the Menhirs, following the coast for 2kms and then turning inland.

POINTE de la TORCHE – excellent spot for coastal walking, and there are also marked circuits here, including a very long one (30kms) on almost level terrain (Circuit de la Pointe de la Torche).

MAHALON – from the village, there is a 12km marked circuit to the lake of Poulguidou and the chapel of St-Tugdual. For a shorter walk, park near the chapel at Lambabu and walk to the lake from there.

TRÉMÉOC – to the west of Tréméoc is the lake of the Moulin Neuf, which has a circular walking trail.

POINTE du MILLIER – exceptional coastal walking, and the wooded valley of the Moulin de Keriolet, with two menhirs.

POINTE du RAZ – superb coastal walking, also a circuit of about 5kms from the parking area to the north coast, then around the point itself and along to the Port de Bestrée before turning back up to the car-park.

OTHER ACTIVITIES

Please note that these lists are intended to provide a good geographical spread of activity providers and are by no means definitive. There are many other establishments all over the department providing similar facilities and expertise.

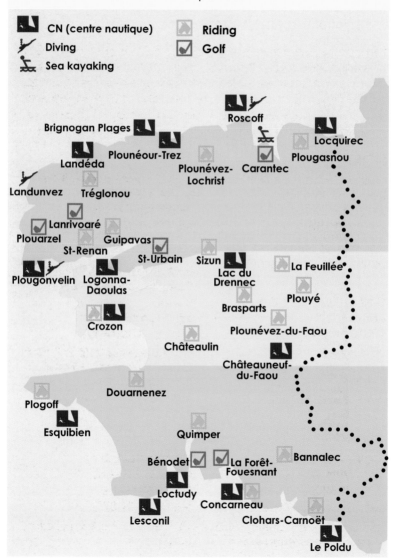

CN (centre nautique)

Diving

Sea kayaking

Riding

Golf

Roscoff

Brignogan Plages

Plounéour-Trez

Landéda

Locquirec

Plougasnou

Plounévez-Lochrist

Carantec

Landunvez

Tréglonou

Lanrivoaré

Plouarzel

St-Renan

Guipavas

St-Urbain

Sizun

La Feuillée

Plougonvelin

Logonna-Daoulas

Lac du Drennec

Plouyé

Brasparts

Crozon

Plounévez-du-Faou

Châteaulin

Châteauneuf-du-Faou

Douarnenez

Plogoff

Esquibien

Quimper

Bénodet

La Forêt-Fouesnant

Bannalec

Loctudy

Concarneau

Lesconil

Clohars-Carnoët

Le Poldu

ACTIVITY HOLIDAYS WITH ACCOMMODATION

For Sail and Stay holidays on the Crozon peninsula, see **www.brittanysail.co.uk**

www.simplybrittany.co.uk has gite holidays in the same area with various sporting activities arranged.

For riding, walking and cycling with gite accommodation near the Monts d'Arrée, see **www.villagebecherel.fr.st**

GOLF

There are some very scenic places to play golf in Finistère, with good quality courses, equipment hire and a wide range of resources. All have practice facilities, shops and refreshments, and lessons are available by arrangement. Anyone is welcome to book and play at these establishments and they are all used to English visitors.

NORTH

Golf de la baie de Morlaix
Route de Kergrist
29660 **Carantec**
tel. 02 98 67 09 14

9 holes (par 34), practice putting and chipping green

Golf de Brest des Abers
Kerhoaden
29810 **Plouarzel**
tel. 02 98 89 68 33

18 holes (par 70), practice facilities
www.abersgolf.com

Golf de Brest Pen ar Bed
Route de St-Renan
29290 **Lanrivoaré**
tel. 02 98 84 98 92

9 holes (par 35)

Brest Iroise Golf Club
Parc des Loisirs de Lann Rohou
29800 **Landerneau**
tel. 02 98 85 16 17

Golf hotel, with 18 (par 71) & 9 (par 37) holes, teaching and practice facilities
www.brest-iroise.com

SOUTH

Golf de Cornouaille
Manoir de Mesneur
29940 **La Forêt-Fouesnant**
tel. 02 98 56 97 09

18 holes (par 71), putting
www.golfdecornouaille.com

Golf de l'Odet
Clohars-Fouesnant
29950 **Bénodet**
tel. 02 98 54 87 88

18 holes (par 72) & 9, practice, putting

CYCLING

Cycling is a major pastime in Finistère and there are many recommended road routes in addition to numerous VTT (mountain bike) trails across varied terrain. Most local tourist boards have produced pamphlets and maps of their territory for cyclists and these are for sale in tourist offices and bookshops. Packs of good quality laminated route cards are reasonably priced at about 5 euros.

Cycle hire (location) is readily available in all areas and tourist offices will be able to provide the relevant information.

Even those who are not regular cyclists may enjoy an amble along the Nantes/Brest canal path or some of the many former railway tracks that now form cycling routes.

PUBLICATION

A Vélo en Finistère is a pack (priced about 4 euros) containing 24 cards of circuits for 'cyclotouristes' all over Finistère. A full map is also included showing all the routes at a glance. Most are between 50 and 60 kms.

This publication, by the departmental tourist board, is available from tourist offices and bookshops.

WEBSITES

www.finisteretourisme.com (printable cycle routes in English)
www.aulne-loisirs.com (cycling on Nantes/Brest canal path)

USEFUL ADDRESS

Comité Départmental de Cyclotourisme
Monsieur Guiffan
47 bis, rue F. le Roy
29000 QUIMPER
tel. 02 98 64 08 64

CONTACTS

There are cycling clubs all over Finistère, with regular outings and organised events. New members are always welcome. The following is a selection:

NORTH

Groupe Cyclotouriste Brestois (Brest) tel. 02 98 03 32 33
Vélo Loisirs Brignogan Plages tel. 02 98 83 43 88
Cyclos Randonneurs du Viaduc (Morlaix) tel. 02 98 88 22 66
C R Landernéens (Landerneau) tel. 02 98 85 33 68

CENTRE

Club Cyclotouriste du Poher (Carhaix) tel. 02 98 93 23 16

Cyclos de l'Aulne (Châteaulin) tel. 02 98 86 18 08

Cyclos et randonneurs de la Presqu'île (Camaret)
tel. 02 98 27 98 77

Les Cyclotouristes Plébennois (Pleyben) tel. 02 98 26 31 07

SOUTH

Cyclos et Randonneurs Concarnois (Concarneau)
tel. 02 98 97 18 37

Cyclos Randonneurs Pont l'Abbistes (Pont l'Abbé)
tel. 02 98 87 24 90

Cyclos et Randonneurs de Cornouaille (Pluguffan)
tel. 02 98 94 00 30

Kemperlé Cyclo Club (Quimperlé) tel. 02 98 96 07 21

The wearing of a helmet is strongly recommended but, at the time of writing, it is not a legal requirement in France.

VTT (Vélos touts terrains)
Individual tourist boards publish their own guides (usually in the form of laminated cards) and these routes are well signed on the ground.
For example:

9 VTT routes on the Crozon peninsula and 10 more for the adjoining territory of Porzay/Ménez Hom
tel. 02 98 27 07 92

4 Explorer trails in Pays d'Iroise – St-Renan
tel. 02 98 84 28 65

40 trails Espace VTT de Cornouaille – Bannalec
tel. 02 98 39 47 00

45 trails in central Finistère – Pleyben tel. 02 98 26 60 25

SIGNAGE
Triangle with two circles beneath it,
usually together with route numbers.
Or VTT and picture of cycle.

RIDING

Finistère is good riding country, with many marked routes, through exceptional scenery. A wide range of equestrian establishments covers all needs, from lessons to trekking.

In addition to organised riding by the day or half-day, there are 54 staging posts across Finistère for those on their own mounts seeking accommodation (for details, see Websites), and many places to stay with several days' riding included.

The balisage (signage) for riders is usually orange. A horse-shoe design with directional markers is used for departmental routes and various symbols for local association circuits.

PUBLICATION: A TOPO Guide with itineraries and much useful factual information is available for purchase from A.R.T.E.B. (Association Régional Tourisme Équitation Bretagne), 27 rue Laennec, 29710 Ploneis (tel. 02 98 91 02 02)

WEBSITES: www.finisteretourisme.com
www.equibreizh.com (whole of Brittany)

USEFUL ADDRESSES

Association Cheval en Finistère, 41 rue Georges Clémenceau, 29400 Landivisiau. tel. 02 98 15 50 43

Comité Régional d'Équitation de Bretagne, tel. 02 97 84 44 00

The following is a selection of riding centres

PC = 'Poney Club' for younger riders
EE = 'École Équitation' with lessons / qualified instruction
CTE = 'Centres de tourisme équestre' for guided rides

NORTH

CTE M. le Vot, Ferme Équestre de Kermébel, 10 route de la Forge, Kermébel, 29630 **Plougasnou**. tel. 02 98 72 33 09

EE/CTE Mme Soler, Ferme Équestre Ranch ar Milin, Beg ar Groas, 29490 **Guipavas**. tel. 02 98 32 12 88

PC/EE/CTE Mme Stéphan, Manoir de Trouzilit, 29870 **Tréglonou**. tel. 02 98 04 01 20

CTE Mme Le Roux / M. Dolci, Poney Ranch de Lescoat, Lescoat, 29430 **Plounévez-Lochrist**. tel. 02 98 61 41 58

CTE M. Bourdon, Les Cavaliers de l'Iroise, Feunteun-Ivin, 29290 **Saint-Renan**. tel. 02 98 84 30 51

CTE Mme Guéguen, Randoloisirs, Kerinizan, 29450 **Sizun**. tel. 02 98 68 89 98

CENTRE

CTE   M Goachet, Village de Bécherel, 29690 **Plouyé**.
tel. 02 98 99 77 24 (unaccompanied riding possible)

EE/CTE   Mme Leseigneur, Centre de Loisirs Équestres,
Kermabilou, 29690 **La Feuillée**. tel. 02 98 99 78 46

CTE   Mme Nicolas, Domaine de Meros,
29530 **Plounévez-du-Faou**. tel. 06 81 02 63 33

PC/EE/CTE Mme Bouchare, Centre Équestre du Rugornou,
Bois du Rugornou, 29190 **Brasparts**. tel. 02 98 81 47 34

PC/EE   M.Berthou, Centre Équestre du Vieux Bourg,
29150 **Châteaulin**. tel. 02 98 16 12 49

PC/EE/CTE   Équitation en Presqu'île, Manoir de Lescoat,
route de Fret, 29160 **Crozon**. tel. 02 98 27 28 05
www.members.aol.com/lescoat

SOUTH

CTE   M. Monfort, Cheval à la Ferme, Cotonard,
29360 **Clohars-Carnoët**. tel. 02 98 39 98 65

CTE   Mme Maugis, Les Randonnées de l'Isole, Boudou,
29380 **Bannalec**. tel. 02 98 39 44 13

PC/EE   Mlle Boitteau, Centre Équestre de Kerguérès,
Chemin de Kerguérès, 29900 **Concarneau**.
tel. 02 98 60 54 52

PC/EE/CTE   Mme Belle, Magic Poney, Le Leuriou, 61 chemin
de Penhoat, 29000 **Quimper**. tel. 02 98 64 39 38
www.members.aol.com/magicpony

PC/EE/CTE   Mme Penfornis, Centre Équestre de Feunteun
Aod, 29770 **Plogoff**. tel. 02 98 70 67 40

PC/EE   Mlle Lebis, Centre Équestre, Ferme de Penfoennec,
29100 **Douarnenez**. tel. 02 98 74 29 72

WATERSPORTS

Finistère, with its fabulous and very varied coastlines, has everything to offer the watersports enthusiast of any age. Some inland locations - the Nantes/Brest canal and Lac du Drennec, for example - are also worth considering.
The schools and centres mentioned here will be able to help with lessons, equipment hire and simple enjoyment of a wide range of watersports activities, such as sailing (including catamarans, canoe-kayaks, etc) wind-surfing, surfing and diving. All have qualified staff for supervised activities and most cater for both adults and children. Booking in advance for courses and hiring equipment is always a sensible precaution, but probably essential at peak holiday periods.

USEFUL WEBSITES
www.nautisme-finistere.com
www.bretagnesailing.com
www.brittanysail.co.uk

CN (centre nautique) = watersports centre
Centre de Voile = sailing centre
École de Voile = sailing school

NORTH

CN Plougonvelin
Boulevard de la Mer
tel. 02 98 48 22 20
(diving arranged)

CN Landunvez
Cale d'Argenton
tel. 02 98 89 54 04
(diving arranged)

**Centre de Voile
L'Aber Wrac'h**
4, port
29870 Landéda
tel. 02 98 04 90 64
www.perso.wanadoo.fr/cvl

Rêves de Mer (This organization has three centres : Plounéour-Trez, Guissény and Santec.)
Le Bourg
29890 Plounéour-Trez
tel. 02 98 83 55 17
www.revesdemer.com

CN de Brignogan Plages
Plage des Crapauds
tel. 02 98 83 44 76
www.perso.wanadoo.fr/centre
nautiquedebrignoganplages

CN Roscoff
Quai d'Auxerre
Roscoff
tel. 02 98 69 72 79

Aquacamp
Diving Centre
Le Ruguel
Roscoff
tel. 02 98 61 09 94

CENTRE
Centre nautique de moulin mer
Logonna Daoulas
tel. 02 98 20 75 00
lmv@moulin-mer.fr

Aulne Loisirs Plaisance
Châteauneuf-du-Faou
tel. 02 98 73 28 63
Boat hire, canoe-kayaks, VTT, VTC

SOUTH
École de Voile les Glénans
Place Philippe Viannay
Concarneau
tel. 02 98 97 14 84
www.glenans.asso.fr

Point Passion Plage
Plage des Sables Blancs
Concarneau
tel. 02 98 50 59 54
(Equipment hire)

Centre International de Plongée des Glenan
tel. 02 98 50 57 02
(diving)

École de Voile
29241 Locquirec
tel. 02 98 67 44 57

Sea-kayaking from
Carantec in the Bay of
Morlaix
tel. 02 98 67 06 13
www.lockayak.com

CN de Crozon-Morgat
Port de Plaisance
29160 Crozon
tel. 02 98 16 00 00
www.crozon-morgat.com/cncm

CN de l'Arrée
Lac du Drennec
tel. 02 98 78 92 91
(weekend activities)
www.asso.ffr.fr/cn-arree

Club nautique du Poldu
tel. 02 98 39 99 41

CN de Loctudy
Plage de Langoz
29750 Loctudy
tel. 02 98 87 42 84
www.cn.loctudy.asso.fr

CN de Lesconil
2 rue Victor Hugo
29740 Lesconil
tel. 02 98 87 89 43

CN Baie d'Audierne
Plage de Ste-Evette
29770 Esquibien
tel. 02 98 70 21 69
www.voile-capsizun.com

FISHING

Fishing is easily accessible in Finistère both on rivers and lakes. Category 1 classification denotes the main salmon and trout waters, and Category 2 includes fine carp and pike fishing.

Permits (cartes de pêche) are required and these can be purchased at designated bars/tabacs, fishing tackle shops, sports' shops, etc. There is an annual licence or a shorter 'Carte Vacance' (30 euros in 2004) which allows 15 consecutive days fishing between June and the end of September, although seasons vary according to the area and type of fish.

Each area has its own association (Maison de Pêche) and the permits are for waters in their control. Regulations and hours will be explained with the permit, and advice on location and the best techniques is usually readily available.

Lakes also require permits. A local mairie will know where permits can be purchased.

Sea fishing is available from various ports around Finistère.

Practical guides are available from Federation de la Pêche, Quimper. Tel. 02 98 10 34 20, fax 02 98 52 15 13, or email: fedepeche29@wanadoo.fr

The following is a list of selected areas, their associations (normally called Association Agrée de Pêche et de Protection des Milieux Aquatiques, or AAPPMA) and outlets for the purchase of permits.

NORTH

The ELORN
The Élorn river is well known for its salmon fishing.
Association tel. 02 98 68 85 08
www.elorn-aappma.com

Permits available from

Maison de la Rivière, Sizun
(general fishing information point here as well as the association's office)

Bar de l'Élorn
Gare
Landivisiau

Le Poisson Volant
16 Rue Général Mangin
Landivisiau

MORLAIX
100kms of trout and salmon rivers.
L'Association Agrée de Pêche et Pisciculture de Morlaix
tel. 02 98 63 33 83 (M. Fournier)

Permits available from
Au fil de l'eau (Philippe le Maux)
7-9 rue de Brest, Morlaix.
tel. 02 98 63 38 80

PAYS DES ABERS
Aber Wrac'h, Aber Benoit, plus lakes
Association tel. 02 98 84 81 59
www.assopeche.com/paydesabers

Permits available from
J-L Salaun, 11 rue de la Mairie, 29870 Lannilis

CENTRE
To fish in the Réservoir de St-Michel, a special
permit/supplement is required from outlets in the Brasparts
or Huelgoat association areas.

HUELGOAT
Association tel. 02 98 99 03 98

Permits available from
Bijouterie Le Borgne, 28 Pl. Aristide Briand, Huelgoat.
Restaurant Le Yeun, Parc d'Entreprises, Brennilis

BRASPARTS
Association tel. 02 98 73 04 88

Permits available from
Maison de la Presse Tabac, 2 rue Quimper, Pont de Buis
Bar Le Mercure, 28 Pl. Charles De Gaulle, Pleyben

CHÂTEAUNEUF-du-FAOU
The Aulne
Association tel. 02 98 73 42 63

Permits available from
Gil' Pêche, 26 rue de la Mairie, Châteauneuf-du-Faou
Café de la Poste, Châteauneuf-du-Faou

SOUTH

QUIMPERLÉ
L'Association de Pêche de Quimperlé
tel. 02 98 39 34 02
Day permit for the Bassin du Bélon
(Annual or 15 day for Laïta, Ellé, Scorff and Bassin du Bélon)

Permits available from
Hervé-Pierre Le Stum, Kervali, Quimperlé
(fishing tackle shop)

ROSPORDEN
Association tel. 02 98 50 92 98

Permits available from
Bar L'Embuscade, 3 rue Reims, Rosporden all year,
camping site and tourist office in summer.

QUIMPER
Association tel. 06 07 06 38 48

Permits available from
Chasse et Pêche Bourhis, 33bis Ave. de la Gare, Quimper
Aquapêche, 36 route Bénodet, Quimper.

SEA FISHING

NORTH
Barabord Club
Roscoff (all year)
M. Diraison
tel. 06 60 09 74 99

CENTRE
Pesketour
1 quai Téphany
Camaret
tel. 02 98 27 98 44

SOUTH
Vedettes Rosmeur
Douarnenez
tel. 02 98 92 83 83

Vedettes de l'Odet
2 avenue de l'Odet
Vieux Port
29950 Bénodet
tel. 02 98 57 00 58

The following may also be of interest:

Musée de la Pêche, Ville Close, Concarneau.
Tel. 02 98 97 10 20

Boat Museum, Port de Rhu, Douarnenez

Yves Joliff, Place de l'Église, Clohars-Carnoët
(shop selling sea fishing tackle)